Toni Morrison

Blackwell Introductions to Literature

This series sets out to provide concise and stimulating introductions to literary subjects. It offers books on major authors (from John Milton to James Joyce), as well as key periods and movements (from Old English literature to the contemporary). Coverage is also afforded to such specific topics as 'Arthurian Romance'. All are written by outstanding scholars as texts to inspire newcomers and others: non-specialists wishing to revisit a topic, or general readers. The prospective overall aim is to ground and prepare students and readers of whatever kind in their pursuit of wider reading.

Published

Toni Morrison

Writing the Moral Imagination

Valerie Smith

WILEY Blackwell

This paperback edition first published 2014
© 2012 Valerie Smith
Edition history: John Wiley & Sons Ltd (hardback, 2012)

Registered Office
John Wiley & Sons Ltd, The Atrium, Southern Gate, Chichester, West Sussex,
PO19 8SQ, UK

Editorial Offices
350 Main Street, Malden, MA 02148-5020, USA
9600 Garsington Road, Oxford, OX4 2DQ, UK
The Atrium, Southern Gate, Chichester, West Sussex, PO19 8SQ, UK

For details of our global editorial offices, for customer services, and for information
about how to apply for permission to reuse the copyright material in this book please
see our website at www.wiley.com/wiley-blackwell.

Library of Congress Cataloging-in-Publication Data

Smith, Valerie, 1956–
Toni Morrison : writing the moral imagination / Valerie Smith.
p. cm. – (Blackwell introductions to literature ; 42)
Includes bibliographical references.
ISBN 978-1-4051-6033-9 (hardback) ISBN 978-1-118-91769-5 (paper)
1. Morrison, Toni–Criticism and interpretation. I. Title.
PS3563.O8749Z856 2012
813'.54–dc23
2012012320

A catalogue record for this book is available from the British Library.

Cover image: Photo of Toni Morrison. © Timothy Greenfield-Sanders

Set in 10/13pt Meridian by Toppan Best-set Premedia Limited
Printed and bound in Malaysia by Vivar Printing Sdn Bhd

1   2014

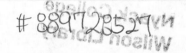

Contents

Acknowledgments

I am grateful to many people and organizations for the intellectual, financial and emotional support I received during the process of writing this book. First and foremost, I thank Toni Morrison for the gift of her eloquent, rigorous, and inspired body of work. Her writing across a wide range of genres has remapped the landscape of African American, US, and global literatures; revised our understanding of our national history; and challenged us to reconsider our understanding of constructions of race, gender, sex, class, and power. I am privileged to have had this opportunity to write a book about one of the most gifted, versatile, and influential writers and intellectuals of our time. I thank her for graciously supporting this project and for spending hours in conversation with me.

I am grateful also to Emma Bennett, Isobel Bainton, Louise Butler, Caroline Clamp, Bridget Jennings, Ben Thatcher, and Kathy Syplywczak at Wiley-Blackwell for their commitment to this project and for their patience and support in seeing it to completion. I thank Alison Waggitt for indexing the book with such care and attention.

I owe a profound debt of gratitude to the Office of the Dean of the Faculty at Princeton University, the School for Historical Studies at the Institute for Advanced Study (IAS), the Guggenheim Foundation, and the Alphonse G. Fletcher Foundation for providing me with support during the years I worked on this book. I am especially grateful to Heinrich von Staden, Professor Emeritus of Classics and History of Science at IAS, for encouraging me to apply to the Institute and for his consistent interest in my project.

The Liguria Study Center in Bogliasco, Italy provided me with space and time to write and revise much of this book. The stunning views of the Ligurian Sea and the spacious, light and airy writing studio and accommodations offered the ideal context in which to work. Special thanks to the gracious, good-humored, and exceptionally efficient staff – Ivana Folle, Alessandra Natale, and Valeria Soave – and the nurturing and brilliant group of fellows – Rosa del Carmen Martinez Ascobereta, Isis Ascobereta, Linda Ben-Zvi, Sam Ben-Zvi, Angela Bourke, Mags Harries, Lajos Heder, Joel Kaye, Erika Latta, Thea Lurie, Michael McMahon, and Roberta Vacca – for creating a vibrant and intellectually stimulating community of friends and colleagues.

I am grateful for the invitations I've received to speak about Morrison's work at colleges and universities both in the US and abroad. I thank Theresa Delgadillo at the Ohio State University; Gillian Logan and Rick Chess at the University of North Carolina, Asheville; Jacquelyn McLendon at the College of William and Mary; Aoi Mori at the Hiroshima Jogakuin University; Azusa Nishimoto at the Aoyama Gakuin University; Sonnet Retman at the University of Washington; and Leslie Wingard at the College of Wooster for allowing me to share my work and to benefit from conversations with their students and colleagues. I also thank Sandra Bermann for inviting me to interview Toni Morrison at a meeting of the American Comparative Literature Association; that conversation provided me with the first opportunity to think about Morrison's books for young readers.

Jessica Asrat, Adrienne Brown, and Nicole Hendrix provided valuable research assistance; I thank these three enormously gifted women for their insight and support. I am also deeply grateful to my friends Evelyn Brooks Higginbotham and Karen Harris and Rob Gips for offering me opportunities to retreat to beautiful places where which I could think, read and write.

Many of the ideas I explore in this book grew out of discussions in the seminars on Toni Morrison I taught both at Princeton and at the Bread Loaf School of English in Asheville, NC. I am grateful to all of the enthusiastic and inspiring students who enrolled in those classes and participated in them which such passion and intellectual fervor, especially: Jessica Asrat, Eli Bromberg, Anna Condella, Alexis Fisher, Diane Humphreys-Barlow, Morgan Kennedy, Genay Kirkpatrick, E. Palmer Seeley, Mike Spara, Candice Weddington, and Mona Zhang.

In *Beloved*, Sixo says of the Thirty-Mile Woman: "She is a friend of my mind." I am blessed to have a community of "friends of my mind." Thank you to Emily Bartels, Lawrence Bobo, Mary Pat Brady, Daphne Brooks, Abena Busia, Benjamin Colbert, Deborah Raikes-Colbert, Theresa Delgadillo, Henry Louis Gates, Jr., Simon Gikandi, William Gleason, Farah Jasmine Griffin, Karen Harris, Evelyn Brooks Higginbotham, Sue Houchins, Tera Hunter, Claudia Johnson, Arthur Little, Marcyliena Morgan, Keidra Morris, Beverly Moss, Dorothy Mullen, Jeff Nunokawa, Carla Hailey Penn, Sonnet Retman, Rita Rothman, Nicole Shelton, Lisa Thompson, Mary Helen Washington, Leslie Wingard, Judi Wortham-Sauls, and Richard Yarborough for the gifts of their intellectual and spiritual companionship.

Finally, I thank my beloved family for their unwavering support for all my endeavors: my dear parents, Will and Josephine Smith; my siblings, Daryl and Raissa Smith, and Vera Smith-Winfree and Glenn Winfree; my "in-laws," Ruth and Walter Winfree; and my nieces and nephews, Alison Smith, Ellis Winfree, Gage Smith and Miriam Smith. I thank Ase Gassaway for his encouragement, companionship, faith and love.

Valerie Smith
July 2012

INTRODUCTION

Toni Morrison ranks among the most highly-regarded and widely-read fiction writers and cultural critics in the history of American literature. Novelist, editor, playwright, essayist, librettist, and children's book author, she has won innumerable prizes and awards and enjoys extraordinarily high regard both in the United States and internationally.[1] Her work has been translated into many languages, including German, Spanish, French, Italian, Norwegian, Finnish, Japanese, and Chinese and is the subject of courses taught and books and articles written by scholars all over the world. It speaks to academic and mass audiences alike; scholars have interpreted her work from myriad perspectives, including various approaches within cultural studies, African Americanist, psychoanalytic, neo-Marxist, linguistic, and feminist methodologies, while four of her novels were Oprah's Book Club selections. She invites frequent comparison with the best-known writers of the global canon: Virginia Woolf, William Faulkner, Zora Neale Hurston, James Joyce, Thomas Hardy, Gabriel Garcia Marquez, Wole Soyinka, Chinua Achebe, and others. Because of her broad appeal, throughout her career, readers and critics alike have sought to praise Morrison by calling her work "universal."

The adjective "universal" has typically been applied to work in any medium that speaks to readers, viewers, or audience members

Toni Morrison: Writing the Moral Imagination, First Edition. Valerie Smith.
© 2012 Valerie Smith. Published 2014 by John Wiley & Sons, Ltd.

whatever their race, ethnicity, gender, sexual orientation, age, or socioeconomic status. Art described as "universal" is contrasted implicitly or explicitly with work that is labeled "provincial," that is, more explicitly grounded in the culture, lore, or vernacular of an identifiable group. But for all its "universality," Morrison's writing is famously steeped in the nuances of African American language, music, everyday life, and cultural history.[2] Even more precisely, most of her novels are concerned with the impact of racial patriarchy upon the lives of black women during specific periods in American history, such as the Colonial period, or the eras of slavery, Reconstruction, Jim Crow, and Civil Rights.

It should not surprise us that Morrison considers the appellation "universal" to be a dubious distinction. In a 1981 interview with Thomas LeClair she remarks:

It is that business of being universal, a word hopelessly stripped of meaning for me. Faulkner wrote what I suppose could be called regional literature and had it published all over the world. It is good – and universal – because it is specifically about a particular world. If I tried to write a universal novel, it would be water.[3]

Here Morrison famously challenges the notion that universal art is unmarred by markers of cultural specificity. Instead, she argues that only by being specific can a work truly be universal. Rather than aspiring to a culturally de-racinated discourse, then, in her fiction she seeks ways of writing about race without reproducing the tropes of racism, or as she puts it in a 1997 essay entitled "Home": "How to be both free and situated; how to convert a racist house into a race-specific yet nonracist home."[4]

As Dwight McBride, Cheryl A. Wall, and others have argued, one way to understand Morrison's career is to consider the interconnections among her roles as writer of fiction and nonfiction, editor, and teacher.[5] On numerous occasions she has herself eschewed the distinction between scholarship or criticism and the creative arts, as for example, she writes in a 2005 essay:

It is shortsighted to relegate the practice of creative arts in the academy to the status of servant to its scholarship, to leave the practice of creative arts along the edge of the humanities as though it were an afterthought, an aspirin to ease serious pain, or a Punch-and-Judy show offering comic relief in the midst of tragedy.[6]

Her adroit use of language notwithstanding, at their core, all of her novels provide astute analyses of cultural and historical processes. Likewise, their critical insightfulness notwithstanding, Morrison's essays and articles make powerful use of narrative and imagery. One never forgets that she is a novelist writing analytic prose or a social and cultural critic writing fiction.

She has been a teacher, editor, critic, and fiction writer, and throughout her career, she has worked in two or more of these areas simultaneously. She taught at a number of colleges and universities while writing fiction, and she published five novels during the period when she both worked as senior editor at Random House and taught. As she continues to produce one path-breaking novel after another, she has also written influential speeches, critical and political essays and articles, libretti, a book of literary criticism, several children's books, and edited two interdisciplinary cultural studies volumes. Moreover, the project of her work outside the realm of fiction writing is tied inextricably to the aims of her fiction itself. To understand the extent of her contributions and achievements, then, it behooves us to consider the nature of those connections.

Throughout her critical writing, Morrison asserts that the role of the reader must be active, not passive; indeed, she suggests that the reader must be actively engaged with the author in a dynamic process out of which textual meaning derives. In "The Dancing Mind," her 1996 acceptance speech delivered on the occasion of receiving the Distinguished Contribution to American Literature Award from the National Book Award Foundation, she writes:

> Underneath the cut of bright and dazzling cloth, pulsing beneath the jewelry, the life of the book world is quite serious. Its real life is about creating and producing and distributing knowledge; about making it possible for the entitled as well as the dispossessed to experience one's own mind dancing with another's; about making sure that the environment in which this work is done is welcoming, supportive.[7]

In part, this view of the relationship between reader and writer reflects the influence of other forms of cultural production and performance, such as dance, oratory, and jazz, upon her work. As she observes in an essay entitled "Rootedness: The Ancestor as Foundation"(1984), in her writing she seeks to inspire her reader to respond to a written text as she or he would to a worship service or a musical performance:

> [Literature] should try deliberately to make you stand up and make you feel something profoundly in the same way that a Black preacher requires his congregation to speak, to join him in the sermon . . . that is being delivered. In the same way that a musician's music is enhanced when there is a response from the audience. Now in a book, which closes, after all – it's of some importance to me to try to make that con-nection – to try to make that happen also. And, having at my disposal only the letters of the alphabet and some punctuation, I have to provide the places and spaces so that the reader can participate. Because it is the affective and participatory relationship between the artist or the speaker and the audience that is of primary importance, as it is in these other art forms I have described.[8]

This quality of engagement is also important to her work because it is a means through which she dismantles the hierarchies that under-gird systemic forms of oppression. For Morrison, language and discur-sive strategies are not ancillary to systems of domination. Rather, they are central means by which racism, sexism, classism, and other ideolo-gies of oppression are maintained, reproduced, and transmitted. As a writer, she may not be inclined or equipped to intervene in the policy arena to bring about social change, but she seeks to use her artistic talents to illuminate and transform the ways in which discursive prac-tices enshrine structures of inequality: "eliminating the potency of racist constructs in language is the work I can do."[9] For this reason, Morrison does not spoon-feed meaning to her readers. For her fiction to serve the function she intends, the reader must be willing to re-read, to work. Hence her novels refuse to tell us overtly what they mean:

> [Her novels other than *Sula*] refuse the 'presentation': refuse the seductive safe harbor; the line of demarcation between the sacred and the obscene, public and private, them and us. Refuse, in effect, to cater to the diminished expectations of the reader, or his or her alarm height-ened by the emotional luggage one carries into the black-topic text.[10]

Elsewhere she has written: "I want my fiction to urge the reader into active participation in the non-narrative, nonliterary experience of the text, which makes it difficult for the reader to confine himself to a cool and distant acceptance of data. . . . I want to subvert [the reader's] traditional comfort so that he may experience an unorthodox one: that of being in the company of his own solitary imagination."[11]

The opening of *Beloved*, for example, unsettles the reader epistemologically in order to invoke the slaves' experience of dislocation. Similarly, the reader of *A Mercy* is likely to be confused by references and allusions to events that have yet to unfold; our disorientation enacts the confusion of the novel's seventeenth-century characters making their way within a world that will become the United States of America.

Moreover, in her fiction and criticism alike, she considers the strategies by which racial ideologies are constructed, maintained, and circulated. One of her most famous essays, "Unspeakable Things Unspoken: The Afro-American Presence in American Literature" (1989), provides the framework of her influential book-length study, *Playing in the Dark: Whiteness and the Literary Imagination* (1992). Here she explores the significance of the silence surrounding the topic of race in the construction of American literary history. For her, many critics' refusal to acknowledge the role of race in the making of the US literary canon exemplifies the unspeakability of race in American culture. To her mind, custodians of the canon retreat into specious arguments about quality and the irrelevance of ideology when defending the critical status quo against charges of racial bias. Moreover, Morrison is skeptical about arguments based on the notion of critical quality, given that aesthetic judgments are inevitably subjective, often self-justifying, and contested.

In this essay she also reflects upon some of the ways in which scholars of African American literature have responded to attempts to delegitimize black literary production. While some critics deny the very existence of African American art, African Americanists have rediscovered texts that have long been ignored, underread, or misinterpreted; have sought to make places for African American writing within the canon; and have developed innovative strategies of interpreting these works. Other critics dismiss African American art as inferior – "imitative, excessive, sensational, mimetic . . . and unintellectual, though very often 'moving,' 'passionate,' 'naturalistic,' 'realistic,' or sociologically 'revealing.'"[12] Those critics, Morrison notes, often lack the acumen, inclination, or commitment to understand the complexity of African American literature. In response to such judgments, African Americanists have mobilized and interpreted recent theories and methodologies (such as deconstruction, psychoanalysis, feminism, and performance theory, to name a few) in relation to African American texts in order to intervene in current critical discourses and debates. Morrison also sharply criticizes those who seek to ennoble African American art by assessing it in relation to the ostensibly universal criteria of Western art. She remarks that such comparisons fail to do justice both to the inherent qualities of the texts and to the myriad traditions of which they are a part.

She describes three strategies critics might utilize in order to undermine such efforts to marginalize African American art and literature. To counteract such assaults on forms of black cultural production, she first proposes that critics develop a theory of literature that responds to the tradition's vernacular qualities: "one that is based on its culture, its history, and the artistic strategies the works employ to negotiate the world it inhabits" (p. 11). Second, she suggests that the canon of classic, nineteenth-century literature be reexamined to illuminate how the African American cultural presence is expressed even in its ostensible absence from white-authored, ostensibly race-neutral texts. Third, she recommends that contemporary literary texts, whether written by white authors or authors of color, be studied for evidence of this presence.

"Unspeakable Things" centers on the second and third strategies; here, Morrison seems intrigued with the rich possibilities contained in the idea of absence:

> We can agree, I think, that invisible things are not necessarily "not-there;" that a void may be empty, but it is not a vacuum. In addition, certain absences are so stressed, so ornate, so planned, they call attention to themselves; arrest us with intentionality and purpose, like neighborhoods that are defined by the population held away from them. (p. 11)

Her incisive reading of Herman Melville's *Moby-Dick* as a critique of the power of whiteness exemplifies the second strategy she outlines and indicates the subtext of race that critics of that classic text long ignored. She demonstrates the third strategy by analyzing the opening sentence of each of her novels to suggest ways in which African American culture becomes legible in black texts. Morrison's readings of her own prose display the acuity of her critical sensibility and her use of language to reveal the subtleties of African American cultural life.

Her book-length critical study, *Playing in the Dark: Whiteness and the Literary Imagination* (1993), is now widely understood to be an extraordinarily influential contribution to discussions of race and US literature. It expands upon the enterprise of "Unspeakable Things" and explores the impact of constructions of race upon a range of key texts in the American literary tradition. As part of the complex project of this work, Morrison establishes the discourses of race within which texts by Willa Cather, Melville, Edgar Allan Poe, Ernest Hemingway, and others participate. By making explicit the assumptions about race inscribed within the texts upon which she focuses, Morrison reveals the centrality of ideas of whiteness and blackness to the idea of America. As she writes:

> It has occurred to me that the very manner by which American literature distinguishes itself as a coherent entity exists because of this unsettled and unsettling population [Africans and African Americans]. Just as the formation of the nation necessitated coded language and purposeful restriction to deal with the racial disingenuousness and moral frailty at its heart, so too did the literature, whose founding characteristics extend into the twentieth century, reproduce the necessity for codes and restriction. Through significant and underscored omissions, startling contradictions, heavily nuanced conflicts, through the way writers peopled their work with the signs and bodies of this presence – one can see that a real or fabricated Africanist presence was crucial to their sense of Americanness.[13]

In the introductions to her two edited collections, Morrison draws analogies between constructions of race in literature and in real life to explore how strategies of racialization functioned within the discourse surrounding two high-profile cultural events from the 1990s. In "Introduction: Friday on the Potomac," which begins *Race-ing Justice, En-gendering Power: Essays on Anita Hill, Clarence Thomas, and the Construction of Social Reality* (1992), Morrison refers to Daniel Defoe's *Robinson Crusoe* to demonstrate that because of the proliferation of racist and sexist stereotypes, both then-Supreme Court nominee Clarence Thomas and Anita Hill (his former attorney-adviser and special assistant who accused him of sexual harassment) were rendered at once overly familiar and incomprehensible during Thomas's Senate confirmation hearings.[14] Reading the figure of Thomas and the discourse surrounding the hearings in light of Daniel Defoe's *Robinson Crusoe*, she explores some of the historically-grounded patterns of domination, acquiescence, and resistance that are reenacted in contemporary cultural and political debates. As Sami Ludwig has noted, in her introduction, "Morrison takes the binary out of the realm of mere language structure and contextualizes it in a historical realm of human interaction."[15] Likewise, in "The Official Story: Dead Man Golfing," the introduction to *Birth of a Nation'hood: Gaze, Script, and Spectacle in the O. J. Simpson Case* (1997), Morrison reads Herman Melville's "Benito Cereno" in relation to Simpson's 1994 criminal trial for the murder of his ex-wife Nicole Brown Simpson and her friend Ronald Goldman. In her analysis, she explores ways in which raced and gendered national narratives produce an official story that eclipses actual events.

* * *

Toni Morrison was born Chloe Ardelia Wofford on February 18, 1931, in Lorain, Ohio, a multiracial steel town. Her parents and other members of her extended family bequeathed to her both a legacy of resistance to oppression and exploitation and an appreciation of African American folklore and cultural practices. Both sets of grandparents migrated from the South to Ohio in hopes of leaving virulent forms of racism behind and finding greater opportunities for themselves and their children; her maternal grandparents came from Alabama, and her father's family came from Georgia.

The music, folklore, ghost stories, dreams, signs, and visitations that are so vividly evoked in her fiction pervaded Morrison's early life and inspired her to capture the qualities of African American cultural expression in her prose. Indeed, Morrison and her critics alike have described the influence of orality, call and response, jazz and dance in her narratives. Yet the presence of myth, enchantment, and folk practices in her work never offers an escape from the sociopolitical conditions that have shaped the lives of African Americans. Cultural dislocation, migration, and urbanization provide the inescapable contexts within which her explorations of the African American past occur.

Literature also played an important role in her childhood and youth. The only child in her first-grade class who was able to read when she entered school, Morrison read widely across a variety of literary traditions as an adolescent and considered the classic Russian novelists, Flaubert, and Jane Austen among her favorites. She was not exposed to the work of previous generations of black women writers until she was an adult. Her delayed introduction to the work of earlier black women writers does not, to her mind, mean that she writes outside that tradition. Rather, the thematic and aesthetic connections between her work and theirs confirm her sense that African American women writers conceive of character and circumstance in specific ways that reflect the historical interconnections between and among constructions of race, gender, sexuality, class, and region. As she remarks in a conversation with the novelist Gloria Naylor:

> [People] who are trying to show certain kinds of connections between myself and Zora Neale Hurston are always dismayed and disappointed in me because I hadn't read Zora Neale Hurston except for one little story before I began to write. . . . The fact that I never read her and still there may be whatever they're finding, similarities and dissimilarities, whatever such critics do, makes the cheese more binding, not less, because it means that the world as perceived by black women at certain times does exist.[16]

Morrison has observed that although the books she read in her youth "were not written for a little black girl in Lorain, Ohio . . . they spoke to [her] out of their own specificity." Her early reading inspired her later "to capture that same specificity about the nature and feeling of the culture [she] grew up in."[17]

After graduating with honors from Lorain High School, she enrolled at Howard University, where she majored in English and minored in classics and from which she graduated in 1953. She describes the Howard years with some measure of ambivalence. She was disappointed with some features of life at the university, which, she has said, "was about getting married, buying clothes and going to parties. It was also about being cool, loving Sarah Vaughan (who only moved her hand a little when she sang) and MJQ [the Modern Jazz Quartet]."[18]

But she was inspired by her participation in the Howard University Players, a student-faculty repertory troupe that took plays on tour throughout the South during the summers. As Susan L. Blake suggests, these trips enhanced the stories of injustice Morrison's grandparents had told her about their early lives in Alabama.[19]

After Howard, she received an MA from Cornell University in 1955, where she wrote a thesis on the theme of suicide in the works of William Faulkner and Virginia Woolf. She then taught at Texas Southern University in Houston from 1955 to 1957 and for 5 years at Howard, where her courses included the freshman humanities survey that focused on "masterpieces of Western literature from Greek and Roman mythology to the King James Bible to twentieth-century novels."[20] Her students at Howard included one of the future leading figures in African American literary and cultural studies, Houston A. Baker, Jr.; future autobiographer Claude Brown; and the future leader of the Student Non-Violent Coordinating Committee, Stokely Carmichael. While at Howard she married Harold Morrison, a Jamaican architect, in 1958 (they divorced in 1964) and had two sons, Harold Ford and Slade Kevin. During this period she also joined a writers' group, for which she wrote a young story about a young black girl who wanted blue eyes. That story would become the basis of her first novel.

When her marriage ended, Morrison returned to Lorain with her two young sons for an eighteen-month period. Subsequently, she began to work in publishing, first as an editor at L. W. Singer, the textbook subsidiary of Random House in Syracuse, New York, and then as senior editor at the headquarters of Random House in Manhattan. While living in Syracuse, she worked on the manuscript of her first novel at night after her children were asleep. In her conversation with Gloria Naylor, she suggests that work on the novel became a way for her to write herself back into existence:

> I had written this little story earlier just for some friends, so I took it out and I began to work it up. And all of those people were me. I was Pecola, Claudia. . . . I was everybody. And as I began to do it, I began to pick up scraps of things I had seen or felt, or didn't see or didn't feel, but imagined. And speculated about and wondered about. And I fell in love with myself.[21]

She sent part of a draft to an editor who liked it enough to suggest that she finish it. Holt, Rinehart, and Winston published *The Bluest Eye* in 1970.

Although Morrison was not familiar with much writing by other African American writers when she began her first novel, she has had a profound impact upon the careers of a range of black authors. As senior editor at Random House, she edited influential texts in African American cultural and intellectual history, including *Angela Davis: An Autobiography*, Davis's *Women, Race, and Class*, Ivan Van Sertima's *They Came Before Columbus*, and Muhammad Ali's *The Greatest, My Own Story.* Moreover, she brought a number of black writers to that publisher's list, including Toni Cade Bambara, Wesley Brown, Lucille Clifton, Henry Dumas, Leon Forrest, June Jordan, Gayl Jones, John McCluskey, and Quincy Troupe.[22]

As Cheryl Wall argues, one can trace deep connections between Morrison's editorial work and her fiction in several ways. Generally speaking, she and the authors she published sought to preserve the lives, voices and wisdom that have been left out of mainstream histories. Moreover, *The Black Book* (1974) the legendary compendium of ephemera, photographs, songs, photographs, and dream interpretations that she edited, documents the creativity and resilience, suffering and pain of both famous and unknown African Americans during and after slavery. That book contains the article about Margaret Garner's murder of her daughter that inspired *Beloved.*

To date, Morrison's publications include ten novels, six books for children, one short story, one book of literary criticism, one edited and one co-edited volume of cultural criticism, and scores of critical essays, reviews, and articles. In her essays and interviews, she often compares the craft of writing to dance, music, and painting.[23] Her fiction reflects the influence of other art forms, such as jazz, dance, photography, and the visual arts, and she frequently collaborates with other artists. She has written a play, *Dreaming Emmett*, which premiered at the Marketplace Theater in Albany, New York in 1986, song cycles with composers, and the libretto for the opera *Margaret Garner* with music by Richard Danielpour. After premieres in Detroit, Cincinnati, and Philadelphia, *Margaret Garner* was staged in Charlotte, North Carolina, in 2006 and opened at New York City Opera in September 2007.[24]

In fall 2006, the Musée du Louvre in Paris invited her to participate in its "Grand Invité" program, under the auspices of which she curated a month-long series of events on the theme of "The Foreigner's Home." Using Théodore Géricault's painting "The Raft of the Medusa" (1819) as a point of departure, Morrison organized a multidisciplinary program "focused on the pain – and rewards – of displacement, immigration and exile." She participated in readings, lectures and panels, and invited artists and curators from around the world to explore this theme. Highlights included a panel discussion on the subject of displacement and language featuring Morrison, Edwidge Danticat (a US writer born in Haiti), Michael Ondaatje (a Sri Lanka-born writer educated in the United Kingdom and living in Canada), and Boubacar Boris Diop (a Senegalese novelist who writes in French and Wolof); an exhibit that paired drawings by Géricault, Charles Le Brun, Georges Seurat, and Edgar Degas with films and videos that focused on the body; and an installation entitled "Foreign Bodies" inspired by Francis Bacon's last, unfinished portrait. In this last piece, the American choreographer William Forsythe and the German sculptor and video artist Peter Welz produced a dance in which Forsythe, with graphite attached to his hands and feet, performed on a large sheet of white paper: "thus a dance inspired by a drawing became itself a drawing."[25]

Throughout her career Morrison has taught at a number of colleges and universities, including Yale, Bard, the State University of New York at Purchase, and the State University of New York at Albany. From 1988 until her retirement in 2006, she held the Robert F. Goheen Professorship of the Humanities at Princeton University. While at Princeton she taught a range of courses on African American literature and creative writing. As Wall notes, in one course she "tried out the ideas of the Africanist presence in American literature that became the core of her influential volume, *Playing in the Dark*."[26] Out of her interest in the fruits of cross-disciplinary artistic conversation, Morrison also pioneered the Princeton Atelier Project, a program that brings guest artists to campus for intensive, collaborative residencies to work with each other, students, and faculty. Atelier artists have included choreographer Jacques d'Amboise, vocal group Anonymous 4, percussionist Evelyn Glennie, cellist Yo-Yo Ma, novelists A. S. Byatt and Gabriel Garcia Marquez, composer Richard Danielpour, filmmaker Louis Massiah, visual artist Irina Nakhova, singer/songwriter Bernice Johnson Reagan, and theater director Peter Sellars.

In her magisterial Nobel Lecture in Literature, delivered in 1993, Morrison brilliantly interweaves narrative and interpretation to offer a meditation on the power of language and the role of the artist. She opens with the story of an elderly, blind, wise woman and the young people who visit her, seeming to make a mockery of her reputation as a clairvoyant. Knowing that she is unable to see, they ask her if the bird they are carrying is alive or dead. After a long pause, the woman replies: "I don't know whether the bird you are holding is dead or alive, but what I do know is that it is in your hands. It is in your hands."[27] In Morrison's reading, the bird is language and the woman is "a practiced writer" (p. 12). The woman's response to their question "shifts attention away from assertions of power to the instrument through which that power is exercised" (p. 12). She asserts that the future of language, and by extension of humanity, is in their hands.

Morrison uses this story to reflect upon the distinction between language that is dead and language that lives, suggesting that the role of the artist is to keep the word alive in the face of myriad forces – the state, the academy, science, the media – that at their worst are invested in its demise. A dead language is not one that is no longer spoken or used:

> Unreceptive to interrogation, it cannot form or tolerate new ideas, shape other thoughts, tell another story, fill baffling silences. . . . Oppressive language does more than represent violence; it is violence; does more than represent the limits of knowledge; it limits knowledge. (p. 14)

In contrast, language that is alive has the power to represent the richness, the mystery, the contradictions, and the uncertainties of individual and communal lives as they are lived:

> The vitality of language lies in its ability to limn the actual, imagined and possible lives of its speakers, readers, writers. Although its poise is sometimes in displacing experience it is not a substitute for it. It arcs toward the place where meaning may lie. . . . Word-work is sublime . . . because it is generative; it makes meaning that secures our difference, our human difference – the way in which we are like no other life. (p. 20)

The story does not end here, however, for Morrison offers an alternate reading of the encounter between the young people and the elderly woman, this time from the point of view of the young people. What if, she asks, there is no bird; if their visit is not meant to mock but rather to solicit wisdom from her? What are the implications of her choosing the self-protectiveness of her cryptic response over the open-ended possibilities of narrative? The young people need the knowledge gleaned from her experience if they are to carry her legacy into the future. In the end, the woman and the youths reach a moment of mutual understanding, born from the questions the young people ask and the lives from the past they imagine. In the closing words of the speech, the woman says:

> Finally . . . I trust you now. I trust you with the bird that is not in your hands because you have truly caught it. Look. How lovely it is, this thing we have done – together. (p. 30)

This story resonates with the aesthetic values to which Morrison repeatedly returns. It recalls the transactional relationship between artist and reader, for the meaning of the story lies in neither reading alone but in the interaction between the two perspectives on the encounter. It recalls her assertion that an absence is not a void but a type of presence. And it expresses her confidence in the wisdom that emerges from paradox rather than the reliance upon false certainties.

Morrison's insistence throughout her career that our common humanity can be found in the specificity of our individual and cultural differences seems strikingly prescient from the vantage point of the second decade of the twenty-first century. After the election of Barack Obama as President of the United States, pundits and many average Americans alike have been quick to declare that the United States has entered the era of post-racialism.[28] Not only is it naïve to assume that the election of an African American president would mean the end of racism when so many markers of racial inequality still exist,[29] but the urge to cloak oneself (or the nation) in the mantle of "post-race" also betrays an eagerness, if not a desperation, to run from the history and the current state of racial formations in the nation. Those who cling to the notion of "post-race" fail to distinguish between racism on the one hand and, on the other hand, discursive practices that acknowl-edge, analyze, and resist the mechanisms through which processes of racialization are enacted. Moreover, they fail to acknowledge that the history and experience of race and racialization processes can yield more than racist language or a discourse of blame and victimization; they imply that there is something inherently shameful in the very language of racial specificity itself. Throughout her writing, whether in fiction or nonfiction, Morrison shows us that however violent, exploitative, and dehumanizing, the history and experience of racial formations have led to complex and rich emotional, cultural, and artistic responses, responses which artists are uniquely positioned to explore, illuminate, preserve, and represent. As she writes in her essay called "Home:"

As an already- and always-raced writer, I knew from the very beginning that I could not, would not, reproduce the master's voice and its assumptions of the all-knowing law of the white father. . . . If I had to live in a racial house, it was important, at the least, to rebuild it so that it was not a windowless prison into which I was forced, a thick-walled, impenetrable container from which no cry could be heard, but rather an open house, grounded, yet generous in its supply of windows and doors. Or, at the most, it became imperative for me to transform this house completely. (p. 4)

Notes

1 A partial list of her many prizes and awards includes the National Book Critics Circle Award, the American Academy and Institute for Arts and Letters Award, the Robert F. Kennedy Book Award, the American Book Award, the Anisfield-Wolf Book Award in Race Relations, the Pulitzer Prize, the MLA Commonwealth Award in Literature, the Nobel Prize for Literature, the Condorcet Medal (Paris), the Pearl Buck Award, the Rhegium Julii Prize for Literature, the National Book Foundation's Medal of Distinguished Contribution to American Letters, the National Humanities Medal, the Pell Award for Lifetime Achievement in the Arts, the Cavore Prize (Turin, Italy), the United Nations Secretary General Lecturer, and the Amnesty International Lecturer. In 2012, Morrison received the Presidential Medal of Freedom.

2 As she observes, "If my work is faithfully to reflect the aesthetic tradition of Afro-American culture, it must make conscious use of the

characteristics of its art forms and translate them into print: antiphony, the group nature of art, its functionality, its improvisational nature, its relationship to audience performance, the critical voice which upholds tradition and communal values and which also provides occasion for an individual to transcend and/or defy group restrictions." See "Memory, Creation, and Writing," *Thought: A Review of Culture and Ideas* 59 (December 1984): 388–389.

3 Thomas Le Clair, "The Language Must Not Sweat: A Conversation with Toni Morrison," in *Conversations with Toni Morrison*, ed. Danille Taylor-Guthrie, (Jackson: University Press of Mississippi, 1994), p. 124.

4 Toni Morrison, "Home," in *The House That Race Built: Black Americans, U. S. Terrain*, ed. Wahneema Lubiano (New York: Pantheon, 1997), p. 5.

5 See, for example, Dwight McBride, "Toni Morrison, Intellectual," in *The Cambridge Companion to Toni Morrison*, ed. Justine Tally (Cambridge: Cambridge University Press, 2008), pp. 162–174 and Cheryl A. Wall, "Toni Morrison, Editor and Teacher," also in *The Cambridge Companion to Toni Morrison*, pp. 139–150.

6 Toni Morrison, Gayatri Spivak, and Ngahuia Te Awekotuku, "Guest Column: Roundtable on the Future of the Humanities in a Fragmented World," *PMLA* 120 (2005): 717.

7 Toni Morrison, "The Dancing Mind," in *Toni Morrison: What Moves at the Margin: Selected Nonfiction*, ed. Carolyn C. Denard (Jackson, MS: University Press of Mississippi, 2008), p. 190.

8 Toni Morrison, "Rootedness: The Ancestor as Foundation," in *Black Women Writers (1950–1980): A Critical Evaluation*, ed. Mari Evans (New York: Doubleday, Anchor Books, 1984), p. 341.

9 Morrison, "Home," p. 4.

10 Toni Morrison, "Unspeakable Things Unspoken: The Afro-American Presence in American Literature," *Michigan Quarterly Review* 28 (1989): 24.

11 Toni Morrison, "Memory, Creation, and Writing," *Thought A Review of Culture and Ideas* 59 (December 1984): 387.

12 Toni Morrison, "Unspeakable Things Unspoken," p. 9.

13 Toni Morrison, *Playing in the Dark: Whiteness and the Literary Imagination* (Cambridge: Harvard University Press, 1992), pp. 5–6.

14 For an insightful analysis of the underlying ideologies of race, sex, and class that structured the discourse surrounding the Clarence Thomas Senate confirmation hearings, see Lisa B. Thompson, "Spectacle of the Respectable: Anita Hill and the Problem of Innocence," in *Beyond the Black Lady: Sexuality and the New African American Middle Class* (Urbana and Chicago: University of Illinois Press, 2009), pp. 21–42.

15 Sami Ludwig, "Toni Morrison's Social Criticism," in *The Cambridge Companion to Toni Morrison*, p. 127.

16   Gloria Naylor and Toni Morrison, "A Conversation," *Southern Review* 21 (July 1985): 589–590.

17   Susan L. Blake, "Toni Morrison," in *Dictionary of Literary Biography*, Vol. 33, *Afro-American Fiction Writers after 1955*, ed. Thadious M. Davis and Trudier Harris (Detroit, MI: Gale Research Co., 1984), p. 188.

18   Blake, p. 188.

19   Blake, p. 188.

20   Cheryl A. Wall, "Toni Morrison, Editor and Teacher," p. 146.

21   Naylor and Morrison, "A Conversation," p. 576.

22   As Cheryl Wall observes in her thoughtful study of Morrison as teacher and editor: "No other editor before Morrison or since has boasted a comparable list of African American writers. As an editor, she helped to define two decades of African American literary history." Cheryl A. Wall, "Toni Morrison, Editor and Teacher," p. 139.

23   See, for example, "Memory, Creation, and Writing"; "The Dancing Mind"; and "The Art of Fiction CXXXIV: Toni Morrison," interview by Elissa Schappell and Claudia Brodsky Lacour, *Paris Review*, 35 (Fall 1993): 82.

24   Her collaborations with composers include: "Honey and Rue," a cycle of six songs commissioned by Carnegie Hall for Kathleen Battle with music by Andre Previn; "Four Songs" with music by Andre Previn premiered by Sylvia McNair; "Sweet Talk" written for Jessye Norman with music by Richard Danielpour; "Spirits in the Well" written for Jessye Norman with music by Richard Danielpour; and "Woman.Life.Song" commissioned by Carnegie Hall for Jessye Norman with music by Judith Weir. In 2011, Morrison's collaboration with director Peter Sellars and composer Rokia Traoré entitled *The Desdemona Project* was performed in Vienna, Brussels, Paris, Berkeley, New York and Berlin; in 2012 it was performed in London. This production is a response to Shakespeare's *Othello* that focuses on the relationship between Desdemona and Barbary, her African nursemaid.

25   Alan Riding, "Rap and Film at the Louvre? What's Up with That?" *The New York Times*, November 21, 2006. Web May 2, 2010.

26   Wall, p. 146.

27   Toni Morrison, *"The Nobel Lecture in Literature, 1993* (New York: Alfred A. Knopf, 1993), p. 11. Subsequent references will be to this edition.

28   For example, after President Obama's first State of the Union address on January 27, 2010, MSNBC commentator Chris Matthews remarked: "I was trying to think about who [Obama] was tonight. It's interesting: he is post-racial, by all appearances. I forgot he was black tonight for an hour. You know, he's gone a long way to become a leader of this country, and past so much history, in just a year or two. I mean, it's something we don't even think about. I was watching, I said, wait a minute, he's an

African American guy in front of a bunch of other white people. And here he is president of the United States and we've completely forgotten that tonight – completely forgotten it. I think it was in the scope of his discussion. It was so broad-ranging, so in tune with so many problems, of aspects, and aspects of American life that you don't think in terms of the old tribalism, the old ethnicity. It was astounding in that regard. A very subtle fact. It's so hard to talk about. Maybe I shouldn't talk about it, but I am. I thought it was profound that way." "Chris Matthews: 'I Forgot Obama Was Black For An Hour,' " http://www.huffingtonpost.com/2010/01/27/chris-matthews-i-forgot-o_n_439701.html, April 26, 2010.

29 I have in mind such factors as persistent gaps in black and white educational achievement and wealth and racially disparate incarceration rates, to mention but a few examples.

CHAPTER 1

The Bluest Eye and Sula

The Bluest Eye

The Bluest Eye (1970), Morrison's first novel, juxtaposes two moments in twentieth-century US culture. The novel centers on a set of traumatic events in the life of Pecola Breedlove, a young African American girl, in the 1940s. Claudia MacTeer, Pecola's friend and the principal narrator, reflects upon these events both from her childhood point of view and from her adult perspective in the late 1960s. In its heightened attention to the politics of aesthetics, *The Bluest Eye* is certainly born out of the racial self-consciousness of the 1960s. But the novel also evokes the advantages and liabilities black migrants from the South encountered as they adapted to their new lives in the North (in this case, Lorain, Ohio) in the mid-twentieth century. In seeking wider opportunities for themselves and their children, they escaped the most virulent forms of racial oppression. But they risked becoming alienated from the values and practices that had sustained previous generations of African Americans.

In *The Bluest Eye*, this sense of alienation is most powerfully expressed in the form of racial self-loathing. Many of the characters have internalized the effects of the selfsame hegemonic social and political policies and practices that brutalized them; they display not only a contempt for African features and social practices associated with black culture, but also a reverence for standards of beauty associated with whiteness.

Toni Morrison: Writing the Moral Imagination, First Edition. Valerie Smith.
© 2012 Valerie Smith. Published 2014 by John Wiley & Sons, Ltd.

Furthermore, the roots of their self-disgust lie so deep that they do not recognize them for what they are. Instead, they project those feelings upon the most vulnerable members of their community, in this case the young Pecola. By the end of the novel, she has been destroyed not only by her rape at the hands of her father, but by the abuse that members of her community heap upon her as well.

In her "Afterword," published in 1993, Morrison describes the moment from her childhood out of which the novel grew. When an elementary school friend expressed a desire for blue eyes, the young Morrison feigned sympathy, but was actually "violently repelled" by the mere idea of the radical alteration of her friend's appearance: "very blue eyes in a very black skin."[1] She recalls that when she heard her friend's wish, she realized for the first time that "Beauty was not simply something to behold; it was something one could *do*" (p. 209). Years later, she still wondered about "the gaze that had condemned" (p. 211) her friend and that her friend had subsequently internalized. *The Bluest Eye* offers a poignant and distilled exploration of the impact of dominant standards of beauty upon those who fall short of those cultural norms. By examining the pernicious effects of racial self-loathing upon the characters, the novel reveals ways in which African American communities are implicated in the valorization and circulation of these aesthetic ideals and the qualities they have come to symbolize.

The novel actually begins three times, a harbinger of the multiplicity of perspectives from which it is told. Before the narrative actually starts, the book opens with an excerpt from a Dick and Jane primer, one of a series of Basic Readers published by Scott, Foresman and Company from 1930 until the late 1960s. These primers both taught generations of children to read through the introduction and repetition of simple words, and also established as normative an idealized vision of a suburban, nuclear, middle-class white family. The second beginning, in italics, is told from the perspective of the adult Claudia. It identifies the year when the events of the novel occurred, mentions Pecola's tragic circumstances, and introduces some of its dominant metaphors, such as seeds and earth. The third beginning, told from Claudia's childhood perspective, actually launches the narrative.

The excerpt from the primer reads as follows:

Here is the house. It is green and white. It has a red door. It is very pretty. Here is the family. Mother, Father, Dick, and Jane live in the green-and-white house. They are very happy. See Jane. She has a red dress. She wants to play. Who will play with Jane? See the cat. It goes meow-meow. Come and play. Come play with Jane. The kitten will not play. See Mother. Mother is very nice. Mother, will you play with Jane? Mother laughs. Laugh, Mother, laugh. See father. He is big and strong. Father, will you play with Jane? Father is smiling. Smile, Father, smile. See the dog. Bowwow goes the dog. Do you want to play with Jane? See the dog run. Run, dog, run. Look, look. Here comes a friend. The friend will play with Jane. They will play a good game. Play, Jane, play. (p. iii)

This excerpt is repeated twice; the first time with no punctuation, no capitalization except for the initial "H," and with the lines spaced closer together. The second time, all the words are run together, and the space between lines has been decreased even further.

The transformation of the passage from a familiar text to the frenzied rush of letters serves multiple functions. First, the excerpt establishes the standard against which Morrison's characters are measured, measure themselves, and are found lacking. Second, it prompts readers to take notice of a passage so familiar that one might overlook it. With neither punctuation, spaces between words, nor capitalization, the passage teeters on the brink of meaninglessness, and the standard of value it articulates and circulates is exposed as arbitrary. And third, the concatenation of letters in the second repetition anticipates the action of the novel, since many of the touchstones of the passage factor into Pecola's traumatic decline: the house, the family, the cat, the dog, the friend. Read in light of her own family circumstances, as well as her encounters with Maureen Peal, Junior, Geraldine, and Soaphead Church, the repetition of the word "play" becomes more than a way of introducing a new vocabulary word. Here it imitates the relentless pressure Pecola feels from standards of value she will never attain. Indeed, the final version is emblematic of Pecola's psychological deterioration; by the end of the novel she is shattered by her own sense of shame and by the self-loathing that others project upon her.

Although *The Bluest Eye* centers on Pecola, Morrison chose not to tell the story from her point of view because, as she writes: "the weight of the novel's inquiry on so delicate and vulnerable a character could smash her and lead readers into the comfort of pitying her rather than into an interrogation of themselves for the smashing" (p. 211). Moreover, by expanding her focus to encompass an entire community,

Morrison ensures that her reader will understand that Pecola's story is far from idiosyncratic. Not only are there three narrators – Claudia MacTeer as both an adult and a child as well as an omniscient narrator – but the text also includes the backstory of the children and adults who have a hand in Pecola's psychological wounding and who are wounded themselves. In projecting their internalized self-loathing onto a child, they exemplify how "the demonization of an entire race could take root inside the most delicate member of society" (p. 210).

The structure of *The Bluest Eye* underscores the proliferation of stories and of narrative voices within the novel. The body of the text is divided into four chapters (each named for a different season of the year) that are, in turn, subdivided. Each chapter begins with an episode, usually involving Pecola, told from the point of view of Claudia the child but shaped by her adult reflections and rhetoric. Claudia's accounts are then followed by one or two stories told by an apparently objective, omniscient narrator. This narrator usually recalls information to which Claudia would not have had access: she tells stories from Pecola's life that involve other characters and weaves flashbacks from these other lives into Pecola's story. In addition, in each chapter, several garbled lines from the primer separate Claudia's voice from the omniscient narrator's and foreshadow the tensions contained within the story that follows.

The chapters juxtapose the 1940s, the eternal present of the primer, and the 1960s. The different narratives and moments in each chapter provide variations on a particular theme; these stories address indirectly the consequences of desiring qualities and possessions that will always be unattainable. By using this technique of repetition with a difference, Morrison reveals the interconnectedness of human lives and the inextricability of past and present. The structure of the novel suggests that readers must place Pecola's story within the context of systemic social practices and beliefs in order to comprehend it.

Claudia MacTeer is strong and self-assertive. Her household comprises a nuclear family that includes her parents, her sister Frieda, and herself, and yet it, too, departs from the hegemonic norm described in the primer: their house is old and cold, not white and green. The MacTeers share the home with roaches, mice, and briefly with a predatory boarder, not with a cat and dog. Unlike the mother in the primer, Mrs. MacTeer does not laugh much. She is a quick-tempered woman who does not mince words when she confronts either a large or small offense. But Claudia recalls the healing presence of her family during a childhood illness: her sister sang a sentimental song to comfort her, and her mother forced her to swallow Vicks salve and massaged the ointment into her chest to help her breathe. From her adult perspective, Claudia appreciates these gestures. She looks back on her childhood and sees that while her experience may not have conformed to the Dick and Jane ideal, she was surrounded by love:

> Love, thick and dark as Alaga syrup, eased up into that cracked window. I could smell it – taste it – sweet, musty, with an edge of wintergreen in its base – everywhere in that house. It stuck, along with my tongue, to the frosted windowpanes. It coated my chest, along with the salve, and when the flannel came undone in my sleep, the clear, sharp curves of air outlined its presence on my throat. And in the night, when my coughing was dry and tough, feet padded into the room, hands repinned the flannel, readjusted the quilt, and rested a moment on my forehead. So when I think of autumn, I think of somebody with hands who does not want me to die. (p. 12)

This passage exemplifies the power of memory to render space symbolic, and the power of narrative to resist hegemonic norms. Through Claudia's eyes, the love that surrounded her transformed the material deprivations of her childhood home into expressions of comfort and security. Her home may have failed to live up to the ideal presented in the primer, but it comes to life in the form of cold wind seeping through a cracked window, the smell of Vicks salve, the sensation of a hot flannel cloth on her neck and chest.

During the fall of 1940 when the novel begins, Pecola and her family are temporarily homeless because Cholly, the alcoholic father, has accidentally set their house afire. Until the family can find a new place to live, the County places Pecola with the MacTeers. Claudia is too young to worship the ideal of beauty that white dolls and little white girls embody and that so many of the black people around her adore. But she is old enough to sense the power they wield over not only Frieda and Pecola, but over the adults in her community as well. Indeed, the seeds of Claudia's power as a narrator are evident in her childhood behavior and preferences. She disdains the white dolls that adults and older girls worship and expect her to value and believes that they have usurped the adoration that rightfully belongs to her.

Instead of treasuring these symbols of white femininity, Claudia takes them apart in hopes of uncovering the mystery of their power.

The MacTeers may fail to fulfill mainstream ideals of a happy family, and they may succumb to the worship of white beauty, but they are able to create an undeniably loving home for their children. In contrast, Pecola's parents, Pauline and Cholly Breedlove, carry deep wounds from their earlier lives, and they take out their frustrations on their children and on each other. Born and raised in Alabama, Pauline found "the end of her lovely beginning" at the age of two, when she stepped on a rusty nail; the wound festered, leaving her with a damaged foot and a limp. To her mind, this deformity explains why she alone lacks a nickname (even her own children call her "Mrs. Breedlove"); why there are no stories about her to secure her place in family memories; and "why she never felt at home anywhere, or that she belonged anyplace" (p. 111). Without a place in the family's oral lore, she found comfort in quiet and solitude, and especially in organizing her own possessions and those of her employers.

She meets Cholly after her family migrates to Kentucky, and he initially fulfills her fantasies for a rich intimate and romantic life. But after they move to Ohio, their marriage deteriorates, at least in part, because of her inability to find and establish community and friendships in the north. A child of the segregated south, she is unaccustomed to living in close proximity to whites, of whom she is afraid. Moreover, other black women scorn her country ways, and Cholly comes to resent her emotional dependency and her financial demands on him. Out of frustration, he turns to drink, and their quarrels grow increasingly violent.

Eventually, Pauline can only satisfy her fantasies of romantic love by imagining herself inside the Hollywood world of make-believe order and beauty. Ironically, she confronts the hollowness of her dream and the disjuncture between her fantasies and her lived experience in a movie theater. Watching a Jean Harlow film, her hair styled like Harlow's, she bites into a piece of candy and accidentally extracts a tooth. The loss of her rotten tooth awakens her to the depths of her own despair; from that moment on, she lets everything go – her appearance as well as her housekeeping – and embraces what she believes to be her own ugliness. Finding solace only in her devotion to respectability, she dedicates herself to a church "where shouting is frowned upon (p. 126)," and to maintaining the home of the Fishers, the prosperous white family for whom she works. With the Fishers she can throw herself into her love of order; there she finds beauty, fastidiousness, and approbation. With them, she even finds her only nickname, "Polly."

Pauline's self-contempt is powerfully in evidence during the scene in which Pecola and the MacTeer sisters stop by to see her at the Fishers'. When Pecola accidentally spills a freshly baked deep-dish berry cobbler all over the floor her mother has just cleaned, scalding her bare legs with the hot juice, Mrs. Breedlove slaps her repeatedly; her tirade makes clear that the floor and the little white Fisher girl are more important to her than her own daughter. She speaks to Pecola with words Claudia describes as "hotter and darker than the smoking berries," but as she comforts the Fisher girl, "the honey in her words complemented the sundown spilling on the lake" (p. 109).

Cholly is likewise trapped in his traumatic past; unable to make peace with his own suffering, he destroys his own life and the lives of those around him. As a child he was abandoned by his parents but raised by his loving Great Aunt Jimmy in Georgia. His downward spiral begins during his adolescence; on the day of Aunt Jimmy's funeral, grief, sex, and racial violence converge. Numbed and confused by the loss of his aunt, Cholly leaves the family gathering after the burial with some of his teenaged cousins to wander in the woods. When he is about to lose his virginity with his cousin Darlene, two white hunters discover them. Turning Cholly's and Darlene's sex play into blood sport, they hold the teenagers at gunpoint; the men leave when they realize that Cholly and Darlene are too humiliated to reach their climax.

In the days to come, Cholly finds that he cannot hate the white hunters. Instead, he directs his hatred toward Darlene, the witness to his humiliation and the person he failed to protect. He goes to Macon in search of the father who had abandoned him only to be harshly rebuffed. Only then does he realize how deeply he misses Aunt Jimmy. While she was alive, he did not know how to respond to her physicality and was often repelled by the smell and appearance of her aging body. But alone on the streets of Macon, when he remembers the very things that he had once found disgusting – her asafetida bag, gold teeth, purple head rag, crooked fingers – he is overcome with grief, for those very characteristics and possessions remind him of what he lost when she died.

Cholly's upbringing failed to prepare him for the responsibilities of family life. The sight of Pecola scratching the back of her calf with her toe reminds him of the way Pauline stood the first time he saw her. The structure of the narrative suggests that because of his past deprivations, he does not know what to make of his daughter's vulnerability. The only response available to him is sexual, and thus, in his drunken stupor, he rapes her.

As the adult Claudia explains, black people relegated to a marginal position in Jim Crow culture were hungry for home ownership and prided themselves excessively on maintaining their surroundings. Renters like the Breedloves occupied a lower position on the social hierarchy than owners. And those like Cholly, who through their personal weaknesses lose even the homes they rent, placing their families "outdoors," have positioned themselves "beyond the reaches of human consideration" (p. 18).

Indeed, the home the Breedloves rent expresses the traumatic environment within the family. They live in a building designed to be a storefront, a retail establishment that has been barely repurposed to serve as a residence. By the 1960s, their former home has become a store; before that it was a pizza parlor where young men congregated; before that the building was a Hungarian bakery; and before that a family of gypsies used it as "a base of operations" (p. 34). Before that, the Breedloves lived there. Each subsequent use of the property on the southeast corner of Broadway and Thirty-fifth Street in Lorain is steeped in local lore – the young men congregated there; the Hungarian baker was famous for his pastries; and the girls in the gypsy family, clad in their elaborate dresses, hid "the nakedness . . . in their eyes"(p. 34). In contrast to these vivid accounts preserved in the folklore of the community, the Breedloves have left a minimal impact. The "realtor's whim" in which they live lacks private spaces and contains rooms that do not serve the purpose for which they were designed. Their furniture is randomly distributed, and no one has privacy. Worse, the furniture lacks any of the positive associations that animate personal possessions in memory and the imagination. Any associations the furniture does carry are negative, reminders of shameful transactions or encounters that permeate the space.

Pecola lives in a brutal environment, but she possesses a rich inner life and astute powers of perception that have the power to buoy her spirit. For instance, she displays a glimmer of confidence and pride when she admires the dandelions and cracks in the sidewalk she sees on her way to Yacobowski's store to buy candy. But on her way home from the store, after she has been humiliated by the contemptuous way Yacobowski treats her, she can only see in the dandelions and the crack in the sidewalk an image of the ugliness she believes others see when they look at her. It would be better if she were angry, for anger presumes "an awareness of worth" (p. 50). But instead, she feels shame, for she has internalized the contempt that others feel for her. On the verge of tears, she gets no comfort from her identification with the dandelions and the cracks – she can now only see them as others perceive them – as weeds and defects. Instead, she soothes herself with the candy she has bought – Mary Janes, a sticky sweet candy named for the little blond-haired, blue-eyed white girl whose image appears on the wrapper.

Pecola fetishizes blue eyes because for her, they are both a window into "a world of clean comfort" (p. 50), and an emblem of unattainable beauty. Just as she drank vast quantities of milk out of the Shirley Temple cup at the MacTeers' home in hopes of becoming Shirley Temple, so too does she consume the candy in hopes that she can escape her own body, her own life, and become Mary Jane. Indeed, when her parents fight, Pecola prays to disappear; through the power of her imagination, she feels her body parts disappearing, except for her eyes. Since she cannot make her eyes disappear, she cannot eliminate her power of visual perception and thus she cannot believe herself to be invisible. She has come to believe that if her eyes were beautiful, then she would be different, and so she prays for blue eyes.

The second chapter of the novel, "Winter," exemplifies the way Morrison connects structure and content. At the beginning of "Winter," Claudia recalls the images of security that she and her family associate with the season. Her memories invoke the presence of her father and the home remedies that kept the threat of cold away. The events Claudia and the omniscient narrator describe in this chapter remind us of "pneumonia weather" (as it is called in the vernacular) – warmth that turns abruptly cold. Claudia describes a day on which she is doubly disappointed; the omniscient narrator describes how Pecola is wounded by a woman she longs to become.

Their triumph over a gang of bullies briefly binds the MacTeer sisters, Pecola, and Maureen Peal together. Claudia and Frieda MacTeer usually scorn Maureen, "the high-yellow dream child with long brown hair"(p. 62), but the three of them join forces to protect Pecola from a group of boys who tease her about her dark skin and taunt her about her father's sleeping habits. As the narrator observes, the qualities the boys mock in Pecola are the ones of which they are ashamed in their own lives. Indeed, their insults are one of many examples of the kind of scapegoating to which Pecola is subjected in her community, where people project their self-hatred onto her.

The MacTeers' friendship with Maureen turns out to be short-lived; companionability quickly gives way to jealousy, and the girls begin to fight with each other. The MacTeer sisters cannot forgive Maureen the possessions and characteristics they envy: her wealth, long hair, and fair skin. Her conversation reflects her self-absorption and sense of entitlement and makes them uncomfortably aware of their own proximity to Pecola's condition of deprivation. When they lash out at Maureen, she resorts to the most powerful weapon in her arsenal, her disgust for their dark skin: "I *am* cute! And you ugly! Black and ugly black e mos. I *am* cute!" (p. 73).

When the MacTeer girls arrive home that afternoon, they find momentary consolation from their parents' boarder, Mr. Henry, who is all too ready to cheer them with money for candy and ice cream. For the second time that day their delight turns to sadness, however, for they discover that Mr. Henry has sent them off not out of generosity but out of self-interest: he wants to be free to entertain a pair of prostitutes known as China and the Maginot Line. They thus become unwitting partners in maintaining a sexual secret, one that haunts them later when Mr. Henry molests Frieda. Their betrayal by both Maureen and Mr. Henry reveals how vulnerable they are outside of the safety of their immediate family.

This chapter concludes with the omniscient narrator's account of Pecola's interaction with Junior, one of her black middle-class schoolmates, and his mother, Geraldine. Pecola's encounter with Junior and Geraldine, like her relationship with her own parents, provides a window into the roots of racial self-loathing. Geraldine is part of a wave of upwardly mobile black women who migrated to the north in search of a better life. On the one hand, these women carry a deep love for their past; they "soak up the juice of their home towns and it never leaves them" (p. 81). But on the other hand, in their quest for respectability, they seek to eradicate from their lives many of the qualities they associate with that past, what the narrator calls "the dreadful funkiness of passion, the funkiness of nature, the funkiness of the wide range of human emotions" (p. 83). Obsessed with order, discipline, and cleanliness, Geraldine epitomizes this type of woman. She loves and receives more comfort from her cat than she does either her husband or son, and she associates poor, dark-skinned black children with the "funk" she so desperately needs to escape.

Junior senses that his mother prefers the cat to him; unable to express his anger at her, he directs his rage toward the cat and toward other children. Under the guise of inviting her to play with his cat, he invites Pecola to his home while his mother is out. Awed by the beauty and order of his home, she is caught off guard when Junior shuts her in a room and then tortures (and possibly kills) the cat. When Geraldine returns to find her cat injured, and a dirty, disheveled Pecola in her house, she looks at the child and sees only the markers of impoverished black life she has so energetically sought to escape: the cheap, dirty torn clothing, uncombed hair remind her of the unkempt girls and women of Mobile.

Like Maureen and Mr. Henry, Geraldine represents a false spring. As a young girl in the South, Geraldine was raised to be meticulous, religious, sexless, and unemotional. She is described as if she were a type, not an individual, in order to emphasize the extent of her assimilation; she is so thoroughly socialized and commodified that nothing special or unique about her remains.

The ensuing flashback from Geraldine's point of view explains the vehemence with which she ejects Pecola from her house. Geraldine's adulthood has been a slow process of eradicating "the funk," the disorder and sensory assault she associates with blackness. In Pecola's face she confronts the image of all she has tried to escape and feels as if her private territory has been invaded.

An excerpt from the garbled version of the primer separates Claudia's story from that of the omniscient narrator. Here, as in each of the chapters, these lines comment ironically on the content of the chapter. In "Winter" we read: "SEETHECATITGOESMEOWMEOWCOMEAND PLAYCOMEPLAYWITHJANETHEKITTENWILLNOTPLAYPLAYPLA." The correctly punctuated version of these lines might evoke the cliché of the coy household cat too finicky to play. But the scenario at Geraldine's house to which the lines refer is as jumbled as the lines are themselves. For one thing, as the narrator tells us, the cat has replaced both Geraldine's husband and her son in her affections.

Moreover, the cat is central to the episode the chapter describes. Junior lures Pecola into his house by promising to let her play with his cat. He tortures and perhaps kills the cat when he finds that it and Pecola are drawn to each other. So if Geraldine's cat will not play, it may well be because it is dead.

This chapter thus shows some of the forms that overinvestment in an alien cultural standard may take. Like Pecola, Maureen and Geraldine yearn to be white. Pecola's aspirations are entirely unattainable, since they take the form of a desire for blue eyes. Maureen and Geraldine aspire to intermediate goals that are more easily accessible. But their desires spring from a hatred of what they are that is as profound as Pecola's. By juxtaposing these and other stories to Pecola's, Morrison displays the dimensions of her protagonist's condition.

Soaphead Church, the misanthrope, is the extreme expression of this tendency toward self-loathing. He is introduced as "an old man who loved things, for the slightest contact with people produced in him a faint but persistent nausea" (p. 164). Repelled by the possibility of contact with other people, except little girls, he yearns instead for objects that humans have touched.

Soaphead comes by his racial self-loathing naturally. He is descended from a line of people who marry others of mixed racial parentage in order to distance themselves from their African origins. In Lorain he can be both part of and separate from the rest of the community by serving as a "Reader, Adviser, and Interpreter of Dreams." It is thus no surprise that once she becomes pregnant, Pecola visits him to request blue eyes. He sees in her an "ugly little girl" who "wanted to rise up out of the pit of her blackness and see the world with blue eyes" (p. 174). Instead of helping her, he tricks her into killing his landlady's elderly dog, thus sending her further into madness. This chapter ends with Soaphead's letter to God in which, as John N. Duvall argues, he reveals a modicum of transformation and self-awareness:

> However arrogant and unbalanced he may be, in the act of writing, Church has made a minimal movement from consciousness to self-consciousness; witnessing Pecola's felt revelation serves as Church's own revelatory moment inasmuch as it takes him from a position of nonimplication (his belief that his life allows him to be a witness to 'human stupidity without sharing it or being compromised by it') to one that recognizes his implication.[2]

For all his perversity, Soaphead is insightful. He anticipates the view of the community at which Claudia arrives at the end of the novel when he describes the people he knew back home in the Caribbean:

> We in this colony took as our own the most dramatic, and the most obvious, of our white masters' characteristics, which were, of course, their worst. On retaining the identity of our race, we held fast to those characteristics most gratifying to sustain and least troublesome to maintain. Consequently we were not royal but snobbish, not aristocratic but class-conscious; we believed authority was cruelty to our inferiors, and education was being at school. We mistook violence for passion, indolence for leisure, and thought recklessness was freedom. We raised our children and reared our crops; we let infants grow, and property develop. Our manhood was defined by acquisitions. Our womanhood by acquiescence. And the smell of your fruit and the labor of your days we abhorred. (p. 177)

By the end of the novel, Pecola has suffered a mental breakdown as a result of the trauma she has experienced. In the penultimate section of the book, she is engaged in an intense conversation with someone she calls a friend. But the "friend" to whom she is speaking is her alter ego; we can tell from their exchange that she believes that she now has blue eyes, and that all she wants to do is to admire them in the mirror. We also learn that since Soaphead gave her her blue eyes, no one will meet her gaze.

The adult Claudia remembers Pecola wandering the streets, flailing her arms like a grotesque and wounded bird unable to fly. Claudia rightly realizes that the entire community had failed her. Pecola has not gone mad because of the rape and Soaphead's deception alone. The scapegoating that has played such an instrumental role in the cycle of racial self-loathing has also contributed to her destruction. In language that recalls Soaphead Church's letter to God, Claudia recognizes the hollowness of the community's pantomime of virtue. So thoroughly damaged by the racist regime whose values they have internalized, they are able only to perform the weaker version of the attributes to which they aspire:

> . . . we were not strong, only aggressive; we were not free, merely licensed; we were not compassionate, we were polite; not good, but well behaved. We courted death in order to call ourselves brave, and hid like

thieves from life. We substituted good grammar for intellect; we switched habits to simulate maturity; we rearranged lies and called it truth, seeing in the new pattern of an old idea the Revelation and the Word. (p. 206)

Sula

Morrison's second novel, *Sula*, confounds binary oppositions. As Deborah E. McDowell has observed, in reading this work, "We enter a new world . . . a world where we never get to the 'bottom' of things, a world that demands a shift from an either/or orientation to one that is both/and, full of shifts and contradictions."[3] Indeed, throughout the text, Morrison interrogates the ground upon which individual and collective identities are constructed.

Sula is divided into two sections and then subdivided into chapters entitled by dates ranging from 1919 to 1965. It opens with a prologue narrated from the point of view of the present which tells the story of its setting, a community called the Bottom. The narrator establishes that the novel takes place during a moment in the life of the town when it was animated by black people's music, stories, dance, and rituals. But like many municipalities across the country, Medallion, Ohio (the fictional town within which the Bottom is located) was transformed by urban renewal, part of a national effort during the 1950s through the 1970s to improve so-called blighted areas of cities and towns.[4] Places such as the Time and a Half Pool Hall, Irene's Palace of Cosmetology, and Reba's Grill were leveled to make room for the Medallion Golf Course and the suburbs. *Sula* is thus situated in a place of change and loss. Here the interests of working African American men and women have been displaced in favor of the creation of white leisure cultural spaces.[5]

The narrator goes on to describe the way in which the Bottom, the ironically named community, received its name. In her words, the story is "a nigger joke."[6] A white farmer promised his slave freedom and a piece of bottomland in exchange for performing some laborious tasks. When the time came for the farmer to make good on his word, he tricked the slave into believing that the term "bottomland" actually referred to land in the hills. That land may be high up from a human perspective, the farmer says, but from God's point of view, it is "the bottom of heaven" (p. 5). As it turns out, the land in The Bottom may have been more difficult to farm, but it really was quite beautiful; so much so, in fact, that some people were left to wonder if it really is the bottom of heaven.

As a tale that white people tell about black people and blacks tell about themselves, the story comments upon exploitative labor practices, the violation of property rights, and the strategies of resistance that historically have inflected African American lives. It suggests how blacks have made meaning from practices that seek to disenfranchise and oppress them. Indeed, it anticipates an observation that Morrison makes in an interview with Bessie W. Jones about the relationship between irony as a strategy of resistance in her work:

> Any irony is the mainstay [for black people]. Other people call it humor. It's not really that. It's not sort of laughing away one's troubles. And laughter itself for black people has nothing to do with what's funny at all. And taking that which is peripheral, or violent or doomed or something that nobody else can see any value in and making value out of it or having a psychological attitude about duress is part of what made us stay alive and fairly coherent, and irony is a part of that – being able to see the underside of something, as well.[7]

In addition to emphasizing the place of irony in African American cultural life, this account of the genesis of The Bottom introduces the issue of the instability of meanings that is central to the text as a whole. Indeed, this idea connects the opening description to the story of Shadrack, the shell-shocked World War I veteran, that immediately follows it. Shadrack's mental instability results from his battlefield experience when, surrounded by the sudden eruption of shellfire and explosions, he witnessed the death of one of his fellow soldiers. Wounded himself, he regains consciousness in a hospital bed, but the trauma of this unanticipated devastation both defamiliarizes his own body and its movement through space and impedes his ability to connect words to their meanings. When he reaches for food, for example, his fingers seem to take on a life of their own and grow out of proportion. And when his nurse calls him "private," he wonders why the man refers to him as something secret. After Shadrack returns to Medallion, he is only able to conquer his fear by creating National Suicide Day; devoting the third day of each year to death, he tells the townspeople that "this was their only chance to kill themselves or each other" (p. 14). By relegating death to one day a year, he hopes to avert the power of the unexpected and keep himself and everyone else safe the rest of the time.

The relationship between Shadrack's story and the rest of the novel is not immediately evident. Indeed, the title character does not appear in the novel until the second third of the book. That her story is deferred until the reader is introduced to the town, to Shadrack, to her best friend Nel and Nel's family, as well as to Sula's own family, suggests that like Pecola's story, Sula's is at once individual and collective, part of the fabric of the communal lore of The Bottom.

Like several of Morrison's novels, *Sula* focuses on a cluster of black women characters.[8] Nel and Sula, the central figures, are complementary opposites. The daughter of Wiley Wright, a cook on one of the Great Lakes ships and his beautiful, respectable wife Helene, Nel is the product of a restrained and conservative black middle-class background. She glimpses the vulnerability beneath her mother's composed veneer during their trip to New Orleans after her great grandmother, Cecile Sabat, falls ill. Not only are she and her mother subjected to the indignities of transportation on a segregated train car – an alien experience to a child reared in the north – but Nel shares the disdain of her fellow black passengers when she witnesses her ordinarily dignified mother smile obsequiously at the conductor who upbraids them when he sees them in the whites-only car. When they arrive in New Orleans, they discover that Cecile has already passed away, but in her house they encounter her daughter and Helene's mother, the prostitute Rochelle. Delicate, sweet-smelling, and dressed in a canary yellow dress, Rochelle is the antithesis of her daughter; barely masking her contempt, Helene describes her as "much handled" (p. 27). Nel's experiences on this trip undermine the certainties of her life and awaken in her a sense of her unique identity. Although she never travels outside of Medallion again, the journey expands her sense of possibilities and prepares her for her transformative friendship with Sula.

In contrast to Nel, Sula is the product of a more iconoclastic and adventurous household. Her grandmother, the one-legged matriarch Eva Peace, presides over an idiosyncratically and improvisationally constructed home populated by a motley assortment of "children, friends, strays, and a constant stream of boarders" (p. 30). After her marriage to a man named BoyBoy dissolves, Eva is left alone to raise her three children: Hannah, Eva (called Pearl), and her son Plum.

Unable to support her children on her own, she leaves them in the care of a neighbor; she returns 18 months later with one leg and sufficient means to build a new house and care for her family, fueling rumors that she has sacrificed her limb in exchange for a substantial insurance settlement.

If Nel Wright is known for her respectability, Eva's nonconformity is legendary. She provides a home for the lost, such as Tar Baby, a man reputed to be white with a penchant for alcohol but blessed "with the sweetest hill voice imaginable" (p. 40), and the deweys, three abandoned children she takes in and upon whom she bestows the name Dewey King. She and her daughter Hannah share a quality the narrator refers to as "manlove." Eva does not maintain an active sexual life, but she has many gentleman callers. Hannah, in contrast, sleeps with as many men as she can in order to satisfy her need to be touched every day.

Eva expresses maternal love in ways that are powerful, often violent. She throws herself from a second-story window in a futile effort to smother the flames that consume her daughter Hannah. In a novel replete with wounded male figures – Shadrack, Tar Baby, the perpetually childlike deweys – she saves Plum twice in especially harrowing ways. First, when he was a child, she pulled rock-hard excrement from his anus. The second time takes place after he returns home from the war with a cocaine addiction; despite Eva's best efforts, he is unable to break out of his self-destructive behavior. Powerless to save her son from himself, Eva decides that the only way she can rescue him is to take his life, so she burns him alive.

Heir to this maternal legacy, Sula is more iconoclastic than Nel. Early in their friendship, the two enjoy an intense, almost erotic closeness. As the narrator remarks:

> Daughters of distant mothers and incomprehensible fathers (Sula's because he was dead; Nel's because he wasn't), they found in each other's eyes the intimacy they were looking for. (p. 52)

As lonely preadolescents, each finds in the other what she lacks in order to become fully herself. Moreover, their friendship provides each girl with the comfort she requires in order to begin to understand her sexuality; in each other's company, they brave and secretly enjoy the appraising eyes of the men who congregate on Carpenter's Road.

The novel thus ostensibly revolves around a set of binary oppositions: Shadrach's madness versus the sanity of the ordinary townspeople, and the outlaw Sula versus the more respectable Nel. As events
unfold, however, these contrasts seem less distinct than they initially
appear. The townspeople may think that the ritual of National Suicide
Day is a mark of Shadrack's insanity, but they have comparable ways
of shielding themselves from the unpredictability of evil and loss.
Likewise, for all their differences, Nel and Sula need each other to
develop into maturity and individuality. Indeed, Nel may seem to be
an innocent witness to Sula's extreme behavior – especially the drowning of Chicken Little. But by the end of the novel she is forced to
acknowledge that spectatorship is not an innocent activity, and to recognize that she derived some pleasure from watching the surface of
the water close over his body.

Sula's and Nel's relationship consolidates even more fully after the
drowning death of Chicken Little. Their experience both binds them
together with a shared secret and also problematizes the connections
between looking and doing and between innocence and guilt. The
events leading up to the death of Chicken Little are juxtaposed with,
and might even be the indirect result of, Sula's overhearing her mother
tell a friend that while she loves Sula, she does not like her. The
narrator suggests a connection between these two incidents later on
when she remarks that "the first experience taught her there was no
other that you could count on; the second that there was no self to
count on either" (pp. 118–119).

Shortly after Sula hears her mother's conversation, she and Nel run
to the riverbank. Silently, they begin to play in the grass: each girl
strokes blades of grass and then digs a hole in the dirt with a stick.
After the two holes become one, they fill it with their sticks and other
bits of debris, and cover it with soil and the grass they have uprooted,
burying it all in a makeshift grave. Some critics have interpreted this
scene as a displacement of the girls' sexual energy, a ritualized burial
of their attraction to one another.[9] One might also read the scene as
a pantomime of the death of childhood innocence brought about by
the conversation that Sula overhears. Either way, this scene is part
of a pivotal moment in the girls' personal development, for it leads
to their accidental drowning of Chicken Little. What began as an
innocent childhood game – swinging the young boy out over the water
– turns deadly when Sula loses her grip on him and he sinks into

the river. The girls are stunned both by the fact that in an instant they have taken a life, and by the possibility that someone – namely Shadrack – might have seen them do it. The novel never confirms whether he saw the death of Chicken Little; when he and Sula encounter each other immediately after the drowning, he speaks only one word to her: "Always." She and Nel understand him to mean that he did, in fact, witness the death and that he – and by extension they – will never forget it. But by the end of the novel we learn that he says the word "Always" because it is the only word of comfort he knows to offer to an obviously distressed child. From his own traumatic past experience, he knows only to try to reassure her that she need not fear catastrophic change.

This episode is also significant because it calls into question the distinction between guilt and innocence. At first glimpse it seems obvious that Sula is responsible for Chicken Little's death and that Nel is merely an innocent bystander. However, when Chicken Little disappears under the surface of the water, Nel's first concern is whether "someone saw." Because she is complicit in keeping the cause of his death a secret, her behavior raises the issue of her culpability.

The issue of the ethics of spectatorship also emerges around Hannah's accidental death by fire. Having risked her own life to keep Hannah from burning alive, Eva observes Sula stand by and watch her mother burn, "not because she was paralyzed with fear, but because she was interested" (p. 78). As was the case with Nel and the death of Chicken Little, this episode does not suggest that Sula is responsible for her mother's death; however, it does raise questions about the role of the witness as viewer of another person's suffering or death. Much later in the novel, when Nel visits her in the nursing home, Eva accuses her of throwing Chicken Little in the water. When Nel denies her responsibility and blames Sula, Eva says simply: "You. Sula. What's the difference? You was there. You watched, didn't you? Me, I never would've watched" (p. 168). Not only does Eva deny the distinction between Nel and Sula, but she also denies that watching and doing are substantively different.

Part One of the novel concludes with Nel's marriage to Jude Greene. The wedding is the culmination of Helene Wright's dreams and desires for her daughter; the lavish display also makes it a major event in the life of Medallion. Furthermore, the marriage provides Nel with a source of fulfillment, for at least temporarily it gives her life a purpose.

Although initially she was not especially eager to marry, she was all too ready to assume her role within the racialized patriarchal order once she realized that Jude needed her to help him compensate for the assault that structural racism had perpetrated upon his masculinity. Jude had hoped to be hired to help build the New River Road as part of a wave of prosperity that followed World War I. But the construction company has no place for strong, young black men, only hiring elderly black men to clean, serve food, and run errands. Jude decides, therefore, that he needs a wife to provide him with consolation and comfort. If the world of work will not make him feel like a man, then he expects that being head of his household will do so.

Part Two of the novel begins 10 years after the wedding, with Sula's return in 1937. Her time away has heightened her spirit of rebelliousness. She re-enters her grandmother's house in defiance; within months she has Eva committed to a nursing home for elderly black women. At first, Nel is delighted to have Sula back in her life; for Nel, seeing her again "was like getting the use of an eye back, having a cataract removed" (p. 95). But Sula's disregard for social norms knows no bounds. She sleeps with Jude for no reason other than that he "filled up the space" (p. 144), thereby destroying her friendship with Nel as well as Nel's marriage. Indeed, she seeks to live outside the restraints of prevailing social norms, especially as they are constructed for women:

> Eva's arrogance and Hannah's self-indulgence merged in her and, with a twist that was all her own imagination, she lived out her days exploring her own thoughts and emotions, giving them full rein, feeling no obligation to please anybody unless their pleasure pleased her. As willing to feel pain as to give pain, to feel pleasure as to give pleasure, hers was an experimental life – ever since her mother's remarks sent her flying up those stairs, ever since her one major feeling of responsibility had been exercised on the bank of a river with a closed place in the middle. (p. 118)

Sula's outlaw behavior, which includes sleeping with and discarding the men of Medallion notwithstanding their marital status, actually creates an important role for her within the town. Medallion's black residents view Sula as the source of evil in their world; her presence gives them a way of creating order out of the chaos and random difficulties of their lives.[10] Viewing her as the repository of evil in their lives, they are able to hold themselves to a higher standard of morality. As the narrator observes:

> Once the source of their personal misfortune was identified, they had leave to protect and love one another. They began to cherish their husbands and wives, protect their children, repair their homes and in general band together against the devil in their midst. (p. 117)

Sula may appear to flout the conventions of her society, but in her relationship with Ajax, she too falls prey to the possessiveness commonly associated with heterosexual romantic love. Despite her efforts to improvise a life, she cannot avoid slipping into the roles women traditionally perform in monogamous relationships. This slide into predictability drives Ajax away; and just a few years later she succumbs to a fatal illness. Years after Sula's death, Nel realizes that the sense of longing she has felt since Jude's departure is really a response to losing Sula.

In her first two novels, then, Morrison holds racialized and gendered cultural norms up to scrutiny. In *The Bluest Eye*, she explores processes through which the pursuit of idealized standards of beauty leads to self-loathing and victimizes the most vulnerable members of an already marginalized community. In *Sula*, Morrison delves more deeply into the means by which social norms are produced to interrogate the binary logic upon which they are based and from which they derive their force. The relationship between Shadrack and the town of Medallion on the one hand, and the friendship between Nel and Sula on the other hand, suggest that rather than polar opposites, notions such as madness and sanity, innocence and guilt, respectability and rebelliousness are actually mutually dependent and inextricable constructions. Societies may need to demonize "the other" in order to shore up their own systems of belief, but their very survival depends upon the existence of that "other"; distinctions between insiders and outsiders are shown to be less stable and evident than they initially appear.

Notes

1 Toni Morrison, *The Bluest Eye* (New York: Holt, Rinehart and Winston, 1970; rpt. New York: Plume, 1973), pp. 209–211. Subsequent references will be to this edition.

2   John N. Duvall, *The Identifying Fictions of Toni Morrison* (New York: Palgrave Macmillan, 2000), p. 33.

3   Deborah E. McDowell, " 'The Self and the Other': Reading Toni Morrison's *Sula* and the Black Female Text," ed. Nellie Y. McKay, *Critical Essays on Toni Morrison* (Boston, MA: G. K. Hall, 1988), p. 80.

4   In theory, urban renewal (often ironically called "urban removal") was intended to enhance the landscape of cities and provide displaced residents with improved housing alternatives. In practice, however, many rich and vibrant communities of color were flattened throughout the United States to make way for highways, leisure spaces, commercial enterprises, and multistory buildings. Residents, some of whom were homeowners, were either relegated to substandard public housing or forced to relocate elsewhere. Mindy Fullilove defines this process as "root shock." According to her, root shock is "the traumatic stress reaction to the loss of some or all of one's emotional ecosystem." This devastation of social networks, Fullilove explains, "is a profound . . . upheaval that destroys the working model of the world that had existed in the individual's head that threatens both individual and communal identities." See *Root Shock: How Tearing Up City Neighborhoods Hurts America and What We Can Do About It* (New York: Random House, 2004), pp. 11–14.

5   Barbara Johnson writes powerfully about the Freudian echoes of Morrison's representation of home as a place that both is familiar and has never been. See her essay " 'Aesthetic' and 'Rapport' in Toni Morrison's *Sula*," in *The Aesthetics of Toni Morrison: Speaking the Unspeakable*, ed. Marc C. Conner (Jackson: University Press of Mississippi, 2000), p. 4.

6   Toni Morrison, *Sula* (New York: Knopf, 1973; rpt. New York: Vintage, 2004), p. 4. Subsequent references will be to this edition.

7   Bessie W. Jones and Audrey Vinson, "An Interview with Toni Morrison," in *Conversations with Toni Morrison*, ed. Danille Taylor Guthrie (Jackson: University Press of Mississippi, 1994), p. 175.

8   This is especially true of *The Bluest Eye, Beloved, Paradise, Love*, and *A Mercy*.

9   See, for example, Diane Gillespie and Missy Dehn Kubitschek, "Who Cares? Women-Centered Psychology in *Sula*," in *Toni Morrison's Fiction: Contemporary Criticism*, ed. David Middleton (New York: Garland, 2000), pp. 61–94. As Gillespie and Kubitschek observe: "The scene shows clearly their subconscious recognition of their femininity in their construction of the yonic symbols and their conception of themselves as one (either defined by gender or joined sexually)," p. 84.

10   Indeed, their treatment of Sula recalls Shadrack's use of National Suicide Day to protect him from evil, as well as the scapegoating of Pecola in *The Bluest Eye*.

CHAPTER 2

Song of Solomon
and Tar Baby

Song of Solomon

When *Song of Solomon* was published in 1977, it was enthusiastically received and widely reviewed. Its publication catapulted Morrison into the ranks of the most highly acclaimed contemporary writers; in addition to the National Book Critics' Circle Award, this novel received an American Academy of Arts and Letters Award. In 1980, President Jimmy Carter appointed Morrison to the National Council on the Arts, and in 1981, she was elected to the American Academy of Arts and Letters.

As Morrison herself has observed, *Song* reflects an expansion of her artistic vision and range:

> The challenge of *Song of Solomon* was to manage what was for me a radical shift in imagination from a female locus to a male one. To get out of the house, to de-domesticate the landscape that had so far been the site of my work. To travel. To fly.[1]

A pivotal text in her body of work, it takes up several of the concerns central to her earlier novels (such as the deleterious effects of American cultural norms – especially capitalism and patriarchy – upon African Americans). But rather than focusing on a pair or a trio of young girls or women, this novel centers on several generations of an African

Toni Morrison: Writing the Moral Imagination, First Edition. Valerie Smith.
© 2012 Valerie Smith. Published 2014 by John Wiley & Sons, Ltd.

American family and considers the toll that dominant cultural practices and assumptions have taken on women and men alike. Moreover, with its multigenerational view of the impact of slavery, migration, and racial and economic injustice upon African Americans, it anticipates the breadth and preoccupations of Morrison's later work. Covering the period from slavery until the height of the Civil Rights era, *Song of Solomon* calls our attention to ways in which African Americans sought to articulate and express their identities within the context of historical change and diverse manifestations of social injustice.

Much of the early criticism of *Song of Solomon* addressed the implications of the mystical, supernatural aspects of the novel – Pilate's absent navel, the apparently immortal figure of Circe, Solomon's flight, the oblique ending, for example – reading *Song* as a site of critique of the destructive power of mainstream American cultural values.[2] More recent criticism has emphasized the role of historical and political context in the text.[3] And indeed, with its liberal references to specific institutions such as the Freedmen's Bureau, events such as the first and second World Wars, the murder of Emmett Till, the Montgomery Bus Boycott, the bombing of the Sixteenth Street Baptist Church, or historical figures such as Malcolm X and Martin Luther King, Jr., the novel is clearly situated in the period between Emancipation and the height of the modern Civil Rights Movement. This shift in critical focus has opened up the novel to more complicated and subtle interpretations that view the mythical elements of the novel as symbolic expressions of ways in which African Americans have survived in the spaces within and between the institutions, practices, movements, periods, and grand events that punctuate the official historical record. These more historically-inflected readings have helped to illuminate thematic, rhetorical, and ideological connections between *Song of Solomon* and Morrison's later work.

At its core, *Song of Solomon* is the story of Milkman Dead's unwitting search for freedom and autonomy. Born in an unnamed city in Michigan in 1931, Milkman is the youngest child and only son of a prosperous landlord, Macon Dead, Jr., and his wife, Ruth Foster Dead, the daughter of the town's first African American physician. Macon and his sisters, First Corinthians and "Magdalena called Lena," should be the fulfillment of their middle-class parents' aspirations. But they have all failed to live out the next phase of their parents' American Dream. The daughters are infantilized by the oppressive notions of black womanhood that circulate within their household and community. When they were girls, Macon paraded them around like expensive trinkets to be seen but not touched. Corinthians' Bryn Mawr education equipped her neither for a profession nor for an appropriate marriage. She and her high-strung sister spend their days making velvet roses like two overgrown children until, unbeknownst to her family, Corinthians finds a job as a domestic servant and enters into a relationship with one of her father's tenants.

Despite his parents' expectations, Milkman appears to be destined for a life of alienation from himself and from others because of his preoccupation with his own desires and needs. He cares little about anyone else and looks toward the future for the fulfillment of his hopes and aspirations. But feeling frustrated and trapped, at the age of 32 he journeys to his ancestral home in Virginia to search for the gold he believes is his father's lost inheritance. His journey reverses the traditional African American migration pattern, in which southern black folk left the south to escape the most virulent expressions of white racism and to find greater economic and educational opportunities for themselves and their families in the north. By journeying south, Milkman discovers instead his deep connection to previous generations of his family, and a broader sense of compassion and empathy. Moreover, he comes to understand the passage of time as a cyclical process. When he incorporates both his familial and his personal history into his vision of his own life, he begins to repair his feelings of fragmentation as well as the psychic rupture caused by his family's displacement from the land that had been their home.

*   *   *

The novel begins on the day before Milkman is born, with the suicide of Robert Smith, the insurance agent, who kills himself by jumping off the roof of Mercy Hospital, located on Not Doctor Street. The digression into how Not Doctor Street got its name speaks volumes about the politics of race and ownership, African American psychic dislocation, and the tension between official and vernacular culture in black communities. Although the official name of the street is Mains Avenue, when the only black doctor in the city moved to the street in 1896, his patients started to refer to it as "Doctor Street." Their correspondents in the South began to address letters to them on Doctor Street, and the men who went off to fight in World War I listed their addresses as being on Doctor Street. But after the war, city officials issued a directive indicating that the name "Doctor Street" would no longer be recognized:

> They had notices posted in the stores, barbershops, and restaurants in that part of the city saying that the avenue running northerly and southerly from Shore Road fronting the lake to the junction of routes 6 and 2 leading to Pennsylvania, and also running parallel to and between Rutherford Avenue and Broadway, had always been and would always be known as Mains Avenue and not Doctor Street. (p. 5)

In a gesture of resistance that simultaneously complied with and defied this pronouncement, and that acknowledged and resisted the practices of delegitimization characteristic of Jim Crow segregation, Southside residents began to refer to it as "Not Doctor Street."

As Milkman's story unfolds, we learn about the traumatic effects of slavery and Jim Crow upon his community and his ancestors. Unable to bear the condition of enslavement, his great-grandfather, Solomon, flew back home to Africa, leaving his 21 children behind and his wife, Ryna, to cry for him inconsolably. Macon Dead, Sr., Solomon's son and Milkman's grandfather, a former slave, was an extraordinarily talented man who inspired the other African American men of Montour County, Virginia:

> Macon Dead was the farmer they wanted to be, the clever irrigator, the peach-tree grower, the hog slaughterer, the wild-turkey roaster, the man who could plow forty in no time flat and sing like an angel while he did it. He had come out of nowhere, as ignorant as a hammer and broke as a convict, with nothing but free papers, a Bible, and a pretty black-haired wife, and in one year he'd leased ten acres, the next ten more. Sixteen years later he had one of the best farms in Montour County. (p. 235)

His many gifts notwithstanding, Macon, Sr. is the victim of post-bellum racial injustice. Because he is illiterate, he does not realize until his wife, Singing Byrd, tells him, that the drunken white man with whom he registered at the Freedmen's Bureau in 1869 had entered his place of birth and name incorrectly. Moreover, he is tricked into giving away his farm when he signs a document he cannot read, and he dies trying to protect his land from seizure.

Thrust out on their own abruptly, Macon, Jr. and Pilate eventually choose different strategies for survival. Macon wheels and deals his way into his position as the richest black man in his small city in Michigan. He marries into a wealthy family, acquires property, and makes his fortune renting rooms and houses to poor black people. Milkman can therefore brag about his father's houses, cars, assets, and speculations to the delight of the Reverend Cooper and the other people he meets during his journey to Montour County, Pennsylvania, his father's hometown. The avid materialism and rugged individualism that made Macon financially successful have exacted their price from him in other ways, however. Macon has come to believe that money, property, and keys are the only things that are real; his financial success has cost him his capacity for communication and compassion. The advice he dispenses to his son displays his consummate faith in property and wealth, a faith that causes him to objectify emotion and other people:

> Come to my office; work a couple of hours there and learn what is real. Let me tell you right now that one important thing you'll ever need to know: Own things. And let the things you own own other things. Then you'll own yourself and other people too. (p. 55)

Macon, Jr. believes that a successful businessman cannot afford to be compassionate. Reflecting that his first two keys to rental units would never have multiplied had he accommodated tenants whose rent payments were delinquent, he sees his tenants as property, not people. He brutalizes his wife Ruth both subtly and overtly because he suspects her of incestuous relations with her father and son. Despite his concern for Milkman, he only speaks to him "if his words [hold] some command or criticism" (p. 28). And by refusing to acknowledge Pilate as his sister, Macon denies her humanity as well. His resentment is based in part on his belief that she stole the gold that the two of them should have shared. More significantly, though, he eschews her company because her attire and deportment fail to fulfill mainstream expectations for the conduct and appearance of respectable women.

He fears that his own professional image and relationships with white bankers will be tarnished by any association with his sister, a pants-wearing bootlegger.

Weak and pathetic as she is, Ruth Foster Dead finds subtle methods of objectifying the members of her family as well. She retaliates against her husband's cruelty by manipulating him. Since she cannot attract his attention in any other way, she demeans herself until, out of disgust, he lashes out at her. Similarly, she reflects that she has never appreciated her son's identity as a human being. Before he was born, Milkman was for her "a wished-for bond between herself and Macon, something to hold them together and reinstate their sex lives" (p. 131). After she realizes that her husband will never again gratify her sexually, she uses Milkman to fulfill her needs for physical contact, breastfeeding him until he is four years old.

Indeed, the Macon Deads exemplify the patriarchal, nuclear family that traditionally has been a stable and critical feature not only of American society but also of Western civilization in general. The primary institution for the reproduction and maintenance of children, ideally it provides individuals with the means for understanding their place in the world. But the novel shows repeatedly that the family has failed to provide the support and comfort that the characters require. Solomon flies away and leaves his family behind; Macon's and Guitar's fathers die violently; and even the fathers who remain, like Macon and Dr. Foster, maintain unhealthy relationships with their children. The degeneration of the Dead family and the destructive force of Macon's rugged individualism thus point to the failure of Western hegemonic, patriarchal values. Morrison's depiction of the decline of this family demonstrates the incompatibility of received cultural assumptions with the texture and demands of life in black American communities.[4]

If the Macon Deads seem barren and lifeless, Pilate's family seems more vital and sensual. On his way to his own emotionally empty house one evening, Macon, Jr. peeks through the window of his sister's home in search of spiritual nourishment. He hears the three women singing one song, Pilate stirring the contents of a pot, Reba paring her toenails, and Hagar braiding her hair. Macon is comforted both by the soothing movement of the repetitive actions of each character in the vignette and by the harmony and tranquility of the music they make together.

As Pilate introduces vitality into her brother's life, so does she introduce a life-giving force into the world of Part I of the novel. Her root-working abilities are responsible for Milkman's very existence; her preparations force Macon back into Ruth's bed long enough to impregnate her and stop him from trying to abort the baby. The circumstances of Pilate's birth mark her as a character of larger-than-life dimensions – one who has transcended the limitations of her social and historical location. Since her mother died in childbirth, she essentially delivered herself. Moreover, she was born without a navel; her smooth stomach isolates her from the company of others since those who know of her condition shun her. The absent navel symbolizes her complete independence, suggesting that even as a fetus she did not need to rely on another person for sustenance. Her isolation and self-sufficiency enable her to "throw away every assumption she had learned and [begin] at zero" (p. 149). She is therefore neither trapped nor destroyed by decaying values as her brother's family is. Like Macon she is self-made, but her self-creation departs from, instead of coinciding with, the American myth. Pilate decides for herself what is important to her, and instead of appropriating collective assumptions, she remakes herself accordingly.

Hers is a multigenerational matriarchal household reminiscent of Eva Peace's; like the one-legged Eva, Pilate is marked by a physical absence – in her case her missing navel – that sets her at a distance from her community. Like Eva's (and Macon's, for that matter), Pilate's family declines in power from one generation to the next. Like Eva's daughter Hannah, Pilate's daughter Reba is generous to a fault and loves men indiscriminately, to her detriment. While Pilate and Reba show minimal regard for material possessions, they indulge Hagar to a fault.

Lacking the communal resources she needs to live as an adult woman in the world, Hagar is destroyed when her relationship with Milkman ends. Her monthly cycle of murderous rages gives way to an epic shopping spree when Hagar convinces herself that Milkman no longer loves her because of her appearance. When she returns home she covers herself in clothing and cosmetics that have been ruined in a rainstorm. The hideous spectacle is an outward manifestation of her psychological deterioration; she dies soon afterward. As Katherine Stern has written:

Hagar's death follows so closely on her bid to win back Milkman with new clothes and new makeup that her purchases – Maidenform, Sunny Glow and Mango Tango – seem to blame. Their false promises magnify Milkman's betrayal and deliver the final blow.[5]

Quintessential self-made man that he is, Macon predicates his behavior on a linear conception of time. To his mind, ends justify means; future successes legitimate one's action in the past and in the present and determine the meaning of one's life. Macon's future-oriented perspective is evidenced nowhere more clearly than by his failure to consider his past as part of himself. He denies the importance of his relationship with his sister and of their shared past. Moreover, as he remarks while telling Milkman about his childhood and youth at Lincoln's Heaven (his father's farm in Virginia), he does not even allow himself to think about his past:

> He had not said any of this for years. Had not even reminisced much about it recently. . . . For years he hadn't had that kind of time, or interest. (p. 51)

Macon's linear vision of time is also partly responsible for his sense of family and morality. Because he believes that the meaning and significance of his life are determined by his future successes, he cares only about his son. According to the patriarchal model to which he adheres, it is in that connection that the most important genealogical transfer resides. His wife, daughter, sister, niece are little more than annoyances or inconveniences to him.

Macon's ability to see the world only in linear, exclusive terms explains his lack of sympathy in yet other ways. He excuses his own corruption by considering only the financial profits it brings him. He refuses to extend any compassion to Mrs. Bains (his tenant and the grandmother of Milkman's best friend, Guitar) when she is unable to pay her rent. Such acts of charity are meaningless to him since they will not increase his wealth. And he encourages Milkman and Guitar to steal what he thinks is Pilate's gold, despite the kindness she has shown them all.

In contrast to Macon's, Pilate's vision of time – indeed, of the world – is cyclical and expansive. Instead of repressing the past, she carries it with her in the form of her songs, her stories, and her bag of bones.

She believes that one's sense of identity is rooted in the capacity to look back to the past and synthesize it with the present; it is not enough simply to put it behind oneself and move forward. As she tells Macon:

> You can't take a life and walk off and leave it. Life is life. Precious. And the dead you kill is yours. They stay with you anyway, in your mind. So it's a better thing, a more better thing to have the bones right there with you wherever you go. That way it frees up your mind. (p. 208)

Before Milkman leaves his home in Michigan, he perceives the world in much the same way that his father does. His preoccupation with accumulating wealth and his lack of compassion allow him to abuse the people around him without remorse. For instance, he ends his relationship with Hagar by writing her a letter that reveals little understanding of her feelings despite their years of intimacy. He signs his letter to her "with gratitude," and it is that word and "the flat-out coldness of 'thank you' that drive Hagar to madness" (p. 99).

Macon and Pilate represent alternate means of surviving as African Americans during the era of segregation. Macon thrives as a capitalist within the parallel, Jim Crow economy; Pilate refuses to conform to dominant mores and seeks to live according to her own values and priorities. Guitar Bains is part of a movement that represents a third way, a retributive notion of social justice. Orphaned at an early age, he and his siblings are raised by their grandmother in one of Macon Dead's shacks. As a young man, he joins an organization called the Seven Days that is dedicated to avenging unpunished acts of racial violence by killing random whites in the same manner in which the black person has been killed. By this calculus, they seek to undermine the system of inequality that perpetuates white supremacy. As John Brenkman observes:

> Their revenge was not some form of primitive retribution; it was a groping for justice in a society that cut them off from all legal means of redressing the wrongs done them, even as it fostered violence against their own people. And yet what they mete out is not justice. The Seven Days' vision of evil does not yield a vision of justice but only a hallucinatory racial arithmetic.[6]

Milkman's search for gold indicates further the similarity between his father's vision of the world and his own. He thinks that leaving his hometown, his past, and his responsibilities will guarantee him a sense of his own identity. As he becomes increasingly committed to his and Guitar's scheme to retrieve Pilate's gold, Milkman acquires a clearer but equally false sense of what freedom means. He believes that gold will provide him with the first sense of identity he has ever known.

Milkman's assumption that the key to his liberation will be found in Danville and Shalimar is correct, although it is not gold that will free him. Unbeknownst to him, his journey south becomes a journey towards heightened self-knowledge.[7] In his ancestors' world, communal and mythical values prevail over individualism and materialism; when he adopts their assumptions in place of his own, he arrives at a more complete understanding of what his experience means. When Milkman arrives in the South, he wears an expensive, tasteful outfit: "beige three-piece suit, button down light-blue shirt and black string tie, [and] beautiful Florsheim shoes" (p. 227). He ruins and loses various articles of clothing and jewelry as he looks first for gold and then for the story of his family. Indeed, just before his epiphanic moment in the forest, he has changed from his cosmopolitan attire to overalls and brogans. Similarly, the people he meets in Shalimar force him to throw off his pretenses before they offer him the help and information he needs. Only when he ceases to flaunt his wealth and refer to the women of the community disrespectfully do the men admit him into their circle. Until he sheds the leaden trappings of conspicuous consumption, Milkman is like the peacock he and Guitar see: too weighted down by his vanity to fly.

While he is at home in Michigan, Milkman believes that when he finally achieves his freedom, he will no longer need to submit to the claims of others. In the woods, away the destructive effects of "civilization," he realizes that human connection is an inescapable part of life:

> It sounded old. Deserve. Old and tired and beaten to death. Deserve. Now it seemed to him that he was always saying or thinking that he didn't deserve some bad luck, or some bad treatment from others. He'd told Guitar that he didn't 'deserve' his family's dependence, hatred, or whatever. That he didn't even 'deserve' to hear all the misery and

mutual accusations his parents unloaded on him. Nor did he 'deserve' Hagar's vengeance. But why shouldn't his parents tell him their personal problems? If not him, then who? (p. 276)

While previously he had objectified his friends and relations, thinking only about how they serve his needs, he now empathizes with his parents and reproaches himself for having robbed Pilate. In keeping with this heightened sensitivity to others and to his own personal history, Milkman, cold to Hagar and unwilling to accept responsibility for her in life, understands her posthumously and assumes the burden of her death. He acknowledges the inappropriateness of his letter to her and realizes that he has used her. Moreover, he knows without being told that she has died and he is to blame. As Pilate has carried with her the bones of the man she believes she has murdered, so too does Milkman resolve to carry with him the box of Hagar's hair: a symbol of his newly acquired vision of a past he no longer needs to escape.

Macon, Sr., Milkman's grandfather, was an American Adam, a farmer who loved the land and worked it profitably. Moving north cost Macon, Jr. some of the talent he had inherited from his father; still able to manipulate cold cash, he lost his father's organic connection to the soil. In the south, Milkman, too, seems disconnected from nature. Graceful in the more "civilized" world, he is clumsy when he enters the wilderness. However, he becomes increasingly attuned to nature's rhythms as he grows in self-awareness. During the bobcat hunt, he senses through the contact between his fingertips and the ground beneath him that someone is about to make an attempt on his life. And as he returns to the town, Milkman feels as if he is part of the "rock and soil" and discovers that he no longer limps.

Finally, however, Milkman's discovery of his identity rests not so much in his connection with the earth, or in his ability to understand his own past; these accomplishments only attend his greater achievement – learning to complete, to understand, and to sing the song that contains his family history. Rather than an official story, this song is a site of vernacular knowledge, one whose meanings must be interpreted out of the various misperceptions, improvisations, and mispronunciations that are part of the process of oral transmission. Only when he immerses himself in the community, for example, does he understand that the name Shalimar is a variant of Solomon and is confused with Charlemagne or Shalleemone, or that when his grand-father returned from the dead to repeat the word "Sing" to Pilate, he was not only telling her to sing, but also speaking her mother's name. As John Brenkman remarks:

> Morrison challenges the habit of thinking of cultural heritage exclusively in terms of monuments and masterworks – comparable to the reduction of history to great events and heroic actors. Such a model is acutely inappropriate for the history of a people whose enslavement denied them literacy and whose oppression in the century since Emancipation denied them the material and institutional means of assembling a monu-mental culture. . . . [A vernacular form of cultural heritage] does not thrive on permanent meanings but on fluctuating connections that nonetheless lead back through time and relate individuals to their col-lectivity and its history.[8]

Milkman comes to know fully who he is when he can supply the lyrics to the song Pilate has only partially known. Throughout his life, Milkman has had an inexplicable fascination with flight. Robert Smith's abortive attempt to fly from the hospital roof precipitated his birth. Riding backward makes him uncomfortable because it reminds him of "flying blind, and not knowing where he [is] going" (p. 32). As he approaches Circe's house, he recalls his recurring childhood fantasy of being able to take flight. When Milkman knows the entire song, however, and can sing it to Pilate as she has sung it to others, he can assume his destiny. Flight is no longer a fancy that haunts him, appear-ing unsummoned in his consciousness. He now understands it as a significant action from his ancestral past. Indeed, the ultimate sign of his achievement of identity is his ability to take flight in the way his grandfather did. In the process of assuming himself, Milkman discovers that his dreams have become attainable.

Milkman acquires a sense of identity when he immerses himself in his extended past. He comes full round from the individualism his father represents and advocates. Assuming identity is thus a communal gesture in this novel, as, indeed, Morrison suggests in her earlier novels. Knowing oneself derives from learning to reach back into history and horizontally in sympathetic relationship to others. Milkman bursts the boundaries of his limited, individualistic conception of self, accepting in its place the richness and complexity of a collective sense of identity.

Tar Baby

In several ways, *Tar Baby* (1982) might seem to represent a radical departure from the rest of Morrison's oeuvre. The only one of her novels to be set largely outside of the United States, other than *A Mercy*, it is also the only one in which white characters feature prominently. These differences notwithstanding, *Tar Baby* shares many of the thematic concerns and preoccupations of the novels that precede and follow it. Like *The Bluest Eye, Sula*, and *Song of Solomon*, it explores the residual impact of slavery upon later generations of African Americans and illuminates the deleterious impact of hegemonic cultural norms. Like *Song of Solomon* and *A Mercy*, it displays a sensitivity to the destructive impact of capitalistic forces and enterprises upon the natural world. Moreover, like many of Morrison's novels, it features several characters who have been displaced voluntarily or involuntarily from their homes and suggests that a return to their literal or symbolic place of origin may be the only way for them to achieve a sense of personal, if not cultural self-knowledge.

Much of the novel is set in L'Arbe de la Croix, Valerian Street's estate on the fictional Caribbean island called L'Isle des Chevaliers, an island inhabited primarily by wealthy white Americans and the indigenous black people whose labor they exploit. A successful candy manufacturer, Valerian built this property as a winter home to provide an escape from the weather, pressures, and responsibilities of his life and work in the States. Now retired, he lives there with his wife Margaret, a former beauty queen 20 years his junior, and their faithful, long-serving African American servants, Sydney and Ondine Childs. Valerian promises Margaret, Sydney, and Ondine that they will only be on the island temporarily, and that they will soon return to Philadelphia, but months there have stretched to years. For Margaret, Sydney, and Ondine, the island has become more of a prison than a retreat.

Set in the 1970s, the novel begins during the weeks leading up to Christmas as the family prepares for the holidays. Margaret makes elaborate plans for the homecoming of her only child, her son Michael. Although Margaret is convinced that Michael will arrive, everyone else is skeptical, since in previous years he has failed to appear. Sydney and Ondine's niece Jadine Childs has arrived, however; she occupies a curiously liminal space within the household. Sydney and Ondine adopted her after she was orphaned and raised her as their own. Thus, she both is and is not their daughter. Moreover, because of her abundant beauty and talents, Valerian and Margaret treat her as if she is a surrogate daughter (or in Margaret's case, sister) rather than a relative of their servants; Valerian has even paid for her college education. By the time the novel opens, she has become an American model with an international career who lives in Paris while completing her doctorate in art history at the Sorbonne.

The uneasy stasis of life at L'Arbe de la Croix is disrupted by the discovery that unbeknownst to the Streets and the Childses, Son Green, an African American who has left the cruise ship on which he had been working, has been living under their roof. Ondine has suspected that someone or something has been stealing food; Margaret finds him hiding in her closet. While Ondine and Sydney are initially horrified by his presence, and Margaret wants to have him arrested for attempted rape, Valerian finds him intriguing and invites him to eat at the family table with himself, Jade, and Margaret.

As Michael once again fails to come for Christmas dinner, Son symbolically assumes the role of the prodigal. Son's presence unsettles the tenuous equilibrium of the household and exposes a host of tensions beneath the ostensibly orderly surface. Son's presence leads to the revelation that Margaret abused Michael as a child; that Ondine knew about the abuse but was powerless to stop it; and that Valerian was unaware of what was happening in his own home. In addition, his presence reveals the hierarchies of language, class, and nation that inform the Childses' treatment of the black people on the island such as Gideon (whom they call Yardman) and Marie Thérèse (whom they call Mary) who assist them with the household labor. Moreover, it exposes the unacknowledged hierarchy of race and power that governs the relationship between the Streets and the Childses; Margaret's terror reflects the extent to which the myth of the black rapist has invaded her imagination, notwithstanding her longstanding, ostensibly trusting relationship with Sydney.

The revelation that Margaret has abused her son shatters the family. Valerian is psychologically destroyed and, almost overnight, slips into a physical decline. Where once he had ruled the household imperiously, now Margaret, simultaneously shamed and empowered by the revelation, begins to take charge. Moreover, Sydney and Ondine, who initially had feared that they would lose their jobs for challenging Valerian's decision to fire Gideon and Marie Thérèse and for revealing the secret of Margaret's abuse, eventually assert even greater control over the household.

In the aftermath of the confrontation at the dinner table, Jadine and Son fall into a passionate affair and leave the island together, first to New York City and then to Son's hometown, the all-black community of Eloe, Florida. As their names – Jadine Childs and Son Green – suggest, the two represent the future, the generation that benefited from the sacrifices of the civil rights revolution. Yet neither has yet found his or her place in the world. Jade visits the Childses and the Streets at L'Arbe de la Croix from her home in Paris, but she cannot decide whether she wants to remain in Europe. Likewise, Son is always on the move and has had trouble deciding where he should be throughout his life. As the narrator observes: "In eight years he'd had seven documented identities and before that a few undocumented ones, so he barely knew his original name himself" (p. 139).[9]

The title of *Tar Baby* invokes the African American folktale that, with some variation, circulates in West African, African American, and Anglo-American cultures, was popularized by Joel Chandler Harris and Walt Disney. In the classic tar baby story, a trickster figure such as Brer Rabbit meets a tar baby that has been placed on the road by a white farmer or by other animals. Brer Rabbit greets the tar baby, and when it fails to respond, he strikes and kicks it repeatedly and becomes stuck to it. Brer Rabbit escapes when he convinces his captors that he is terrified of being thrown in the briar patch, which is really his home. He frees himself by playing on their underestimation of his character and runs away, taunting them.[10]

The tensions in the novel are heightened by the historical racial context, brought to mind by the folktale referenced in the title and by the island's own plantation history. *Tar Baby's* radical departures from Morrison's earlier works, in terms of both its transnational setting and the significant presence of white and wealthy characters, expose the restrictions placed on post Civil Rights-era, working-class free blacks' agency by the mobility of their privileged white employers. The island manor house setting and constant threat of forced departures combine to raise the specter of slavery in the otherwise modern context. The Streets' relationship with their servants initially appears to be egalitarian, and the Streets do treat Jade as a daughter. But the posture Sydney and Ondine assume towards their employers, and their deep-seated anxiety about their own status, reveal the precariousness of their position.

In the novel, Son and Jadine, are both associated with the tar baby story. Son might be read as a tar baby to the extent that the other characters cannot escape his touch and are transformed by it. But he refers to Jadine as a tar baby as well, a figure created by white men's institutions to trap black men. Despite, or perhaps because of their differences, Son and Jadine find themselves in a passionate affair; the very differences that would seem to divide them bear an erotic charge in their respective imaginations. Son is seduced by Jadine's cosmopolitan beauty and sophistication; Jadine is compelled by his earthy sensuality. Yet when they escape the turmoil of life on Isle des Chevaliers and move back to the United States together, each is threatened by the other's world. Son cannot fit into Jadine's life in New York:

> He needed the blood-clot heads of the bougainvillea, the simple green rage of the avocado, the fruit of the banana trees puffed up and stiff like the fingers of gouty kings. Here prestressed concrete and steel contained anger, folded it back on itself to become a craving for things rather than vengeance. (p. 221)

For her part, Jadine feels reproached by the communal norms of the black people she meets in Eloe, Florida, Son's hometown, Florida. Her discomfort with them is made especially evident by the fact that when she is left on her own, she cannot sustain a conversation with them. She can relate to them only by photographing them, commodifying these people who are ostensibly her own in much the same way that she, as a model, is commodified by professional photographers.

Moreover, in Eloe, Jadine is haunted by the specter of the Caribbean and Southern black women who are depicted in the novel as being more traditionally female than their cosmopolitan counterparts. After a night of lovemaking with Son, she dreams that a group of black women from her own and Son's past challenge her with their sexuality. Shortly thereafter, Jadine and Son return to New York, where Jadine hopes to convince Son to get an education and enter a profession. Her efforts to change him are no more successful than his attempts to have her fit in at Eloe; Jadine flees first to Isle des Chevaliers and then to Paris. In the Street household, Valerian and Margaret seem to have reached a tentative accord with each other and with the Childses. At the end of the novel, Son arrives on the island in pursuit of Jadine, although it remains unclear whether any reconciliation between them will be possible.

Morrison's critique of L'Arbe de la Croix and the island on which it is located elaborates upon the vision of the destructive potential of capitalism found in her earlier novels. From the opening pages of the first chapter, she links the devastation of the environment to the exploitative labor practices that created the lavish estates and altered the landscape of the island forever. While the birds and fish were threatened by the Haitian laborers who came to build the winter houses and wreaked havoc on their habitat, the champion daisy trees, the river, the climate, and the earth itself all suffered from their violent interventions. As the narrator observes:

> The men had already folded the earth where there had been no fold and hollowed her where there had been no hollow, which explains what happened to the river. It crested, then lost its course, and finally its head. Evicted from the place where it had lived, and forced into unknown turf, it could not form its pools or waterfalls, and ran every which way. The clouds gathered together, stood still and watched the river scuttle around the forest floor, crash headlong into the haunches of hills with no notion of where it was going, until exhausted, ill and grieving, it slowed to a stop just twenty leagues short of the sea. (p. 9)

For their part, the Haitian laborers were not unionized, and thus were deprived of benefits and a living wage. The narrator remarks that they "could not distinguish between craft and art" (p. 10). As a result, they produced a grand and gorgeous home that is faulty in its construction:

> While the panes did not fit their sashes, the windowsills and door saddles were carved lovingly to perfection. They sometimes forgot or ignored the determination of water to flow downhill so the toilets and bidets could not always produce a uniformly strong swirl of water. But the

eaves were so wide and deep that the windows could be left open even in a storm and no rain could enter the rooms – only wind, scents and torn-away leaves. The floor planks were tongue-in-groove, but the hand-kilned tiles from Mexico, though beautiful to behold, loosened at a touch. Yet the doors were plumb and their knobs, hinges and locks secure as turtles. (pp. 10–11)

Valerian uses the island as an escape from his life in Philadelphia; yet, like Margaret, he cannot fully embrace his life there. While she insists on importing foods from the States that are out of season and non-native to the island, Valerian maintains a greenhouse where he can grow his favorite plants and flowers, none of which are indigenous to the island either. Valerian's wealth, power, and gender and racial privilege enable him to live comfortably in this state of impermanence; he can leave at any moment and know that his wife and employees will follow him. But Sydney and Ondine are trapped in a condition of contractual servitude. Neither slave nor fully free, they have no home of their own and nowhere to settle. Ondine would like to remain on the island and claim it as her home, but Valerian and Margaret shut down any discussion of permanence with the formulation: "It can wait till we get home" (p. 13). In telling Sydney that the Streets "should go back home" rather than grow "Northern flowers" on the "equator," she expresses her frustration with their unyielding connection to the North.

Sydney and Ondine may believe that they are socially superior to the black folk on the island like Gideon and Marie Thérèse because they come from the States, speak English, and have access to greater resources. But their position in the Street household indentures them in a way that an independent business owner such as Marie Thérèse, despite her extreme poverty, is not. Her home may be modest, but Marie Thérèse owns it, and she and Gideon feel secure within it.

Near the end of *Tar Baby*, Valerian is forced to come to terms with the painful secret that has threatened his family for decades and that was revealed at Christmas dinner. Because he has actively chosen to remain ignorant of the events that transpired in his own family, he has shielded himself from the knowledge that his wife, Margaret, was abusing their son, Michael. As he sits in his greenhouse, Valerian reflects:

[He] had chosen not to know the real message that his son had mailed to him from underneath the sink. And all he could say was that he did not know. He was guilty, therefore, of innocence. Was there anything so loathsome as a willfully innocent man? Hardly. An innocent man is a sin before God. Inhuman and therefore unworthy. No man should live without absorbing the sins of his kind, the foul air of his innocence, even if it did wilt rows of angel trumpets that cause them to fall from their vines. (p. 243)

Valerian's observation illuminates the motivation for many of the choices he has made throughout his life; he has been driven by the desire to maintain distance from and control over his relationships and his environment. When his disastrous first marriage ended, he chose to marry Margaret simply because of her physical appearance: "She was so young and so unexpectedly pretty he swallowed air and had a coughing fit" (p. 51). He resolved to retire soon after reaching the age of 65, and then leave Philadelphia with his wife and his faithful African American servants, so he can tend to his greenhouse and "sleep the deep brandy sleep he deserved" (p. 55). In his desire to remain shrouded in willed innocence, shielded from his responsibility for others and for the consequences of his actions, Valerian seems an extension of Macon Dead into the transnational context. He is emblematic of an American insularity or isolationism that is often unwilling to acknowledge its implication in global systems of oppression and capital exploitation.

Notes

1 Toni Morrison, "Foreword," *Song of Solomon* (New York: Vintage, 1977), p. xii. Subsequent references will be to this edition and noted by page number only.
2 See, for example, Dorothy H. Lee, "*Song of Solomon:* To Ride the Air," *Black American Literature Forum* 16.2 (Summer 1982): 64–70; Cynthia A. Davis, "Self, Society, and Myth in Toni Morrison's Fiction," *Contemporary Literature* 23.3 (Summer 1982): 323–342; Joseph T. Skerrett, Jr., "Recitation to the Griot: Storytelling and Listening in Toni Morrison's *Song of Solomon*," in *Conjuring: Black Women, Fiction, and Literary Tradition*, ed. Marjorie Pryse and Hortense J. Spillers (Bloomington: Indiana University Press, 1985), pp. 192–202; and Valerie Smith, "The Quest for and Discovery of Identity

in Toni Morrison's *Song of Solomon*," *Southern Review* 21.3 (Summer 1985): 721–732, and reprinted in *Toni Morrison: Critical Perspectives Past and Present*, ed. Henry Louis Gates, Jr. and K. A. Appiah (New York: Amistad, 1993), pp. 274–283.

3   See, for instance, Melissa Walker, *Down from the Mountaintop: Black Women's Novels in the Wake of the Civil Rights Movement, 1966–1989* (New Haven, CT: Yale University Press, 1991), pp. 131–145; John Brenkman, "Politics and Form in *Song of Solomon*," *Social Text* 39 (Summer 1994): 57–82; Marianne Hirsch, "Knowing Their Names: Toni Morrison's *Song of Solomon*," in *New Essays on "Song of Solomon,"* ed. Valerie Smith (New York: Cambridge University Press, 1995), pp. 69–92; Wahneema Lubiano, "The Postmodernist Rag: Political Identity and the Vernacular in *Song of Solomon*," in *New Essays on "Song of Solomon,"* ed. Valerie Smith (New York: Cambridge University Press, 1995), pp. 93–116; Dana Medoro, "Justice and Citizenship in Toni Morrison's *Song of Solomon*," *Canadian Review of American Studies/Revue canadienne d'etudes americaines* 32.1 (2002): 1–15.

4   For a thoughtful discussion of the decline of the family romance as depicted in the novel, see Hirsch, "Knowing Their Names."

5   Katherine Stern, "Toni Morrison's Beauty Formula," in *The Aesthetics of Toni Morrison: Speaking the Unspeakable*, ed. Marc C. Conner (Jackson: University Press of Mississippi, 2000), p. 79.

6   See Brenkman, "Politics and Form in *Song of Solomon*," p. 73.

7   For an interesting argument about Milkman's quest as a journey of initiation and a reverse migration narrative, see Catherine Carr Lee, "The South in Toni Morrison's *Song of Solomon:* Initiation, Healing, and Home," *Studies in the Literary Imagination* 31.2 (Fall 1998): 109–123.

8   Brenkman, p. 68.

9   Toni Morrison, *Tar Baby* (New York: Vintage, 2004), p. 51. Subsequent references will be to this edition and cited by page number only.

10 For a thorough and insightful analysis of the Tar Baby tale and its relationship to the novel, see Craig H. Werner, "The Briar Patch of Modernist Myth: Morrison, Barthes and Tar Baby As-Is," in *Critical Essays on Toni Morrison*, ed. Nellie Y. McKay (Boston, MA: G. K. Hall, 1988), pp. 150–167.

CHAPTER 3

Beloved

Published in 1987, *Beloved* is widely considered to be Morrison's greatest literary achievement, the most celebrated contemporary novel of the slave experience, and one of the most highly acclaimed novels of the twentieth century. Winner of the 1988 Pulitzer Prize for Fiction, in 2006 it was selected as the best work of US fiction published in the previous 25 years.[1] With its central focus on the traumatic effects of slavery, memory, and forgetting upon the African American individual, familial, and collective consciousness, it is most obviously a novel about the past. But it has also been read as a novel about the present: James Berger explores how *Beloved* operates within the "discursive contexts of the 1980s," opposing both neoconservative and Reaganist denials of systemic racism on the one hand and, on the other hand, liberal denials of the cumulative impact of violence and racism within African American communities.[2] Moreover, in a recent article, Dennis Childs argues convincingly that the novel looks to the future; he demonstrates that in its depiction of the slave ship, the plantation, and the chain gang, *Beloved* illuminates the persistence of the "Middle Passage carceral model" from chattel slavery through Jim Crow era convict labor and the contemporary prison-industrial complex.[3]

Beloved has been interpreted from diverse critical perspectives, including feminist, psychoanalytic, neo-Marxist, and critical race

Toni Morrison: Writing the Moral Imagination, First Edition. Valerie Smith.
© 2012 Valerie Smith. Published 2014 by John Wiley & Sons, Ltd.

theory. It has been read as a text about slavery and freedom, mother-hood, the body, the word, history, and memory. The widespread esteem in which *Beloved* is held confirms Morrison's belief that cultur-ally specific narratives can convey universal truths. The novel addresses the impact of the Middle Passage, enslavement and Reconstruction upon African American bodies, and psychological, emotional, and spiritual lives. Yet it also illuminates the central role of the repressed memory of racial violence and its consequences within the broader story of American democracy. Moreover, with its focus on loss, memory, grief, and healing, the novel tells a story that has resonated with readers across the globe.[4]

The plot of *Beloved* grew out of a newspaper account Morrison dis-covered when she was editing *The Black Book* (1974) during her time as a senior editor at Random House. As Cheryl Wall has argued, *The Black Book*, a documentary history of African Americans, has several methodological and theoretical features in common with *Beloved:*

> *The Black Book* represents a model for reconstructing the past that is topological, interactive, and communal. A fictional reimagining rather than a historical reconstruction, *Beloved* shares these same qualities. Both challenge conventional, historical discourse. Both determine to excavate the lives of the anonymous black folk who have been 'disremembered and unaccounted for.' Both reflect what Morrison views as the necessity for black people to find some way to hold on to the useful past without blocking off the possibilities of the future.[5]

Previously published in the *American Baptist* in 1856, the article, "A Visit to the Slave Mother Who Killed Her Child," tells the story of Margaret Garner, a fugitive slave mother from Kentucky who killed her two-year-old daughter and attempted to kill her three other chil-dren in order to prevent them from being captured and returned to slavery. Margaret Garner, her husband Robert, his parents, and their four children, ranging in age from nine months to six years, crossed the Ohio River from Kentucky into Cincinnati, Ohio. In Cincinnati they were captured by a search party. Margaret Garner was caught between the interests of a slave and a free state, for not only was she subject to prosecution under the terms of the Fugitive Slave Law of 1850, but she also faced murder charges in the state of Ohio. Ultimately, the federal judge who tried her case overruled Ohio's right to prosecute her for murder and upheld the Fugitive Slave law instead. The family was returned to Kentucky where their masters sold them to a plantation in Mississippi. The real Margaret Garner died of typhoid fever in 1858.[6]

With its focus on a mother who chooses to kill her child rather than subject her to life as a slave, and who subsequently is treated as a piece of property within the legal system, the story of Margaret Garner is a deeply personal account that nevertheless resonates with the atrocities and political and epistemological paradoxes that underpinned and sustained the system of slavery. Thus, it is not surprising that her story has both lent itself to a wide range of critical approaches and been translated into a number of genres as well. In the nineteenth century, for example, Frances E. W. Harper and Elizabeth Barrett Browning each wrote poems about her, and her story inspired Thomas Satterwhite Noble's 1867 painting, *The Modern Medea*. After *Beloved* was published, Jonathan Demme directed the 1998 film adaptation based on the screenplay by Akosua Busia and Richard LaGravenese and Adam Brooks; Steven Weisenburger wrote a meticulously researched account of Garner's story and its historical context entitled *Modern Medea* (1998); and Morrison as librettist collaborated with composer Richard Danielpour on the opera, *Margaret Garner*.

Morrison has said that once she learned the basic details of Garner's story, she decided not to do further research about her. As a novelist, she preferred to draw on the resources of her imagination to conjure up the implications, motives, and reverberations of the episode:

> I did a lot of research about everything else in the book – Cincinnati, and abolitionists, and the underground railroad – but I refused to find out anything else about Margaret Garner. I really wanted to invent her life.

> I had a few important things. . . . The sex of the children, how many there were, and the fact that she succeeded in cutting the throat of one and that she was about to bash another one's head up against the wall when someone stopped her. The rest was novel writing.[7]

Like numerous other African American novelists in the second half of the twentieth century and the beginning of the twenty-first, here Morrison draws on the freedom denied antebellum writers of slave narratives to mine the complexity of the experience of enslavement.[8]

While former slaves were constrained by genre conventions and the need to legitimate their humanity and moral rectitude, subsequent generations of African American writers have been free to use their imagination to explore the unacknowledged and elusive effects of the institution upon slaves, slaveholders, and their descendants.[9] Moreover, contemporary authors write from a perspective informed and enriched by the study of slave narratives, the changing historiography of slavery, the complicated history of race and power relations in the United States and throughout the world during the twentieth century, and the rise of psychoanalysis and other theoretical frameworks. As Morrison has written:

> It's a kind of literary archeology: on the basis of some information and a little bit of guesswork you journey to a site to see what remains were left behind and to reconstruct the world that these remains imply.[10]

The narrative present of *Beloved* takes place in Cincinnati in 1873, eight years after the end of the Civil War; set during Reconstruction, much of the novel looks back upon the period of slavery. Indeed, by setting the novel during Reconstruction, Morrison invokes the inescapability of slavery, for the very name of the period calls to mind the havoc and destruction wrought during both the antebellum period and the Civil War years. The characters have been so profoundly affected by the experience of enslavement that time and space cannot separate them from its horrors or undo its effects. Morrison coins the term "rememory" – a word that blends "remember" and "memory" and is thus both verb and noun – to capture the persistent presence of the past, a past so vividly alive that it seems to be embodied. As Sethe, the protagonist, observes:

> Someday you be walking down the road and you hear something or see something going on. So clear. And you think it's you thinking it up. A thought picture. But no. It's when you bump into a rememory that belongs to somebody else. Where I was before I came here, that place is real. It's never going away. Even if the whole farm – every tree and grass blade of it dies.[11]

Readers with even a basic knowledge of the institution of slavery in the United States are aware of certain fundamental facts: enslaved persons were counted as their masters' property; their masters' property rights trumped any claims the enslaved person have over his or her offspring or other family members; they were not citizens and for the purposes of representation were considered 3/5 human; they possessed no rights that white citizens were bound to respect, and thus could not own property, vote, enter into contracts, marry, or bear arms; they were forbidden to learn to read and to write; and since they had no access to the rule of law, they could be whipped, raped, and otherwise abused with impunity. Some may assume that enumerating such a list of atrocities is tantamount to comprehending the circumstances under which enslaved persons lived and worked, but Morrison disabuses us of that notion. Rather than merely rehearse the facts, she guides her readers into her characters' inner lives in order to enhance our understanding of the experience of enslavement. The language of the novel both mines the depths of her characters' grief and losses and confronts the limits of language to express traumatic suffering. As Morrison remarks in an interview:

> I wanted it to be truly *felt*. I wanted to translate the historical into the personal. I spent a long time trying to figure out what it was about slavery that made it so repugnant, so personal, so indifferent, so intimate and yet so public.[12]

The novel begins with the following lines:

> 124 was spiteful. Full of a baby's venom. The women in the house knew it and so did the children. For years each put up with the spite in his own way, but by 1873 Sethe and her daughter Denver were its only victims. (p. 3)

"124" refers to 124 Bluestone Road, the house that Sethe, a former slave, shares with her daughter, Denver, and the ghost of her other daughter, the "crawling already" child she killed. Number 124 had once been home also to Baby Suggs, the mother of Sethe's husband Halle (lost and presumed dead), and to Howard and Buglar, Sethe's two sons, but Baby Suggs has died, and fed up with the baby ghost, the two boys have run away. By beginning the novel with a sequence of numbers, Morrison recognizes that she risks discomfiting readers who will not know to what those numbers are meant to refer. But she has written that she opens in this way for a variety of reasons that are crucial to the meaning of the text as a whole. First, it focuses our attention on the house and gives it an identity and a set of characteristics; beginning with this powerful image underscores the significance of home ownership to those who had been denied the right to own property in their former lives. Second, she writes that "there is something about numerals that makes them spoken, heard;" opening with numbers thus establishes the significant role of orality within the text. But perhaps most significantly, this abrupt opening requires the reader to understand immediately that he/she is entering a world populated by people who exist in an extended, if not permanent, state of disorientation. As Morrison observes:

> No native informant here. The reader is snatched, yanked, thrown into an environment completely foreign, and I want it as the first stroke of the shared experience that might be possible between the reader and the novel's population. Snatched just as the slaves were from one place to another, from any place to another, without preparation and without defense. No lobby, no door, no entrance – a gangplank, perhaps (but a very short one).[13]

The trajectory of the plot begins when Paul D, Sethe's and Halle's old friend from the Sweet Home plantation arrives unexpectedly at 124. In short order, he and Sethe renew their friendship, become lovers, and decide to live together. Paul D tries to rid the house of the baby ghost, but his attempt at exorcism only triggers the arrival of a strange, sickly young woman who emerges from the river and calls herself Beloved. She gradually takes over the house and displaces Paul D. First Denver and then Sethe believe that Beloved is the daughter that Sethe killed. Sethe may have been certain in the moment that killing her daughter was preferable to allowing her to return to slavery. But she has never fully recovered from this traumatic event. Denver has never come to terms with the loss of her sister and the knowledge that her mother is capable of taking her own child's life, and Beloved is consumed and defined by an eternal sense of abandonment. Sethe's desire to compensate for taking her daughter's life, and Beloved's need to attach to Sethe is so profound, that Sethe becomes physically taken over by the relationship. Eventually, Denver is compelled to seek help in the world outside her home. The prayers of women in the community exorcise Beloved, and Paul D is then able to return to help Sethe restore herself and move forward into the future.

Sethe and Paul D are both haunted by vivid recollections of slavery they wish to suppress; powerful images complicate whatever assumptions about slavery we bring to the text. For example, we know that slaves did not own their own bodies and could not lay claim to their children, and that enslaved women were subjected to sexual assault. And we know that slaves were considered property, more animal than human. Those assumptions take on a deeper meaning when Sethe and Paul D struggle to tell each other about their last days at Sweet Home. They had grown accustomed to life with the Garners, who treated them as if they were human and allowed them some measure of autonomy. Under their watch, Sethe was allowed to choose her mate and have a family with him, and Halle was able to hire himself out so that he could buy his mother's freedom. But once Mr. Garner died, life at Sweet Home changed dramatically. Mrs. Garner sold Paul F, one of the male slaves, and brought in her brother-in-law, called Schoolteacher, and his two nephews (or sons, Sethe is never sure which) to run the plantation; conditions deteriorated so precipitously that Sethe, Halle, and their children were forced to make plans to flee.[14]

Sethe fights back memories of having had her breast milk stolen by the nephews, "two boys with mossy teeth," while Schoolteacher stood by taking notes; of slaughtering her daughter to prevent her from being taken back into slavery; and of exchanging sex for the engraving on that same daughter's tombstone. For his part, Paul D fights back the memory of seeing Halle, speechless, covering his face in butter after having witnessed Sethe's violation. As Halle was powerless to intervene on Sethe's behalf, so too was Paul D powerless to help Halle, for Paul D had been forced to wear a bit, an instrument of torture that prevented him from speaking and restrained his movements.

While Paul D says that he has sometimes sung about the bit, he has never told anyone about it before he unburdens himself with Sethe. But he cannot forget the humiliation he felt while wearing the bit, when he met the gaze of the barnyard rooster they called Mister, an animal whose autonomy made Paul D doubt his own humanity. Moreover, he tries to suppress the memory of the hardships and humiliations of the chain gang, where he slept buried underground in a narrow wooden box along with 45 other prisoners, his wrists and ankles bound in iron, forced to chain himself to his fellow captives each morning, and fellate any guard who demanded it.

The former slaves' desperate desire for amnesia notwithstanding, the past will not be kept at bay. The past breaks unexpectedly into the narrative to disrupt the forward movement in time; the slightest sensation triggers memories that overwhelm them. Furthermore, the novel turns on the embodiment and appearance of the figure the woman Sethe and Denver believe to be the child Sethe murdered, but who symbolizes as well the souls of the "Sixty Million and More" lost to the slave trade.[15] In the intensity of their connections with each other, and in their various encounters with Beloved, the characters explore what it means for them to confront their past suffering and to take that past with them into the future.

The novel's focus on bodies is evident both in the predominance of scenes of physical suffering and scarred bodies and in the characters' sensory experience of their past: her attempts to forget her enslavement notwithstanding, Sethe's memories come through her body; sensory perceptions set flashbacks in motion. When she washes stinging chamomile sap off her legs, for example, the scent and the sensation propel her back to her life in Kentucky.

Not only are Sethe's memories triggered by physical sensations, but her body is also linked to the past by virtue of the hieroglyphic scars on her back: she wears on her body the signs of her greatest ordeal at the Sweet Home plantation. The story of the brutal handling she endured as a slave – the stealing of her breast milk and the beating that ensued – is encoded in the scars on her back. Those who see her back are rendered speechless by it; the symbolic power and the pain of which they are traces are expressed in the variety of ways that others attempt to read them. Moreover, those who see her scars take shelter in metaphor in their efforts to describe what they see. Amy Denver, the young white girl who saves her and her baby during her escape (and after whom Denver is named) is the first person to witness to the testimony written on her skin. She first traces it gently with her fingers and then names it: she sees on Sethe's back not merely a hideous scar, but a chokecherry tree.

Baby Suggs sees the imprint from Sethe's back on her bedsheets and on the blanket that covers her shoulders; to her they look like "roses of blood" (p. 93). And Paul D, who cannot read the words of the newspaper story about Sethe's act of infanticide, reads her scarred back as a piece of sculpture: "the decorative work of an ironsmith too passionate for display" (p. 17).

Insofar as the characters feel suffering through their bodies, they are healed through the body as well. Sethe is cured three times by healing hands. First, Amy Denver ministers to her body: exposing her back to the open air and covering it with spider webs, and massaging her feet and improvising a pair of shoes out of leaves and fabric. Baby Suggs, an eloquent preacher, is rendered speechless by the "roses of blood." All she can do is soothe the body: "wordlessly the older woman greased the flowering back and pinned a double thickness of cloth to the inside of the newly stitched dress" (p. 93). And finally, in a gesture that is at once aesthetic, erotic, and nurturing, Paul D reads the suffering on her body through his own body:

> He rubbed his cheek on her back and learned that way her sorrow, the roots of it; its wide trunk and intricate branches . . . [He] would tolerate no peace until he had touched every ridge and leaf of it with his mouth, none of which Sethe could feel because her back skin had been dead for years. (p. 17)

Sethe is not the only one who wears her past suffering on her body. After he leaves Sweet Home, for a time Paul D registers in an incessant trembling the humiliation he felt in the presence of Mister, the rooster, and the indignity of being forced to wear the bit, leg irons and handcuffs. No one knew he was trembling, "because it began inside:"

> A flutter of a kind, in the chest then the shoulder blades. It felt like rippling – gentle at first and then wild. As though the further south they led him the more his blood, frozen like an ice pond for twenty years, began thawing, breaking into pieces that, once melted, had no choice but to swirl and eddy. (p. 106)

As a result of having been murdered by her own mother, Beloved is consumed with a yearning to connect with Sethe's body and spirit that cannot be quenched. She tries to drive a wedge between Sethe and Paul D on the one hand, and between Sethe and Denver on the other. This desire is ostensibly what drives her to compel Paul D to have sexual relations with her. But the unintended consequence of this encounter may well be that it helps Paul D to confront the buried pain of his own suffering. His reluctance to examine his past reflects his sense that his secrets are located in what remains of his heart: "in that tobacco tin buried in his chest where a red heart used to be. Its lid crusted shut" (pp. 72–73). However, when Beloved compels him to have sexual relations with her – to encounter her physically – she tells him to touch her "on the inside part" (p. 117). The description of this scene suggests that the act of intercourse with Beloved helps Paul D to re-open his own heart and begin to face the depths of his own suffering:

> She moved closer with a footfall he didn't hear and he didn't hear the whisper that the flakes of rust made either as they fell away from the seams of his tobacco tin. So when the lid gave he didn't know it. What he knew was that when he reached the inside part he was saying, 'Red heart. Red heart,' over and over again. (p. 117)

Early in her life in freedom, Baby Suggs ministers to the black fugitives and former slaves outside Cincinnati. Her message, which transforms the Christian message of self-abnegation and deliverance after death, is meant to heal the broken and suffering bodies of those who endured slavery. As she herself, with legs, back, head, eyes, hands, kidneys, womb, and tongue broken by slavery, has resolved to use her heart in the service of her vast congregation, she yearns to restore the bodies and spirits of her "congregation" through her sermons:

> Here,' [Baby Suggs] said, 'in this here place, we flesh; flesh that weeps, laughs; flesh that dances on bare feet in grass. Love it. Love it hard. Yonder they do not love your flesh. They despise it. They don't love your eyes; they'd just as soon pick em out. No more do they love the skin on your back. . . . So love your neck; put a hand on it, grace it, stroke it and hold it up. And all your inside parts that they'd just as soon slop for hogs, you got to love them. The dark, dark liver – love it, love it, and the beat and beating heart, love that too. (p. 88)

Readers may be inclined to read Baby Suggs's use of the word "heart" metaphorically, to assume that by "heart" she means compassion or capacity for empathetic identification. But in this litany of broken body parts, the word "heart" points to the organ as well as to an emotional resource. In this context, it becomes more difficult to make the leap from the corporeal referent to the metaphysical; such an erasure of the corporeal would be all too close to the expendability of black bodies under slavery. In contrast, Baby Suggs' sermon encourages the former slaves and the reader to linger over the free black body – a body so easily reviled, broken, discarded, assaulted, and commodified while enslaved – and to love it as flesh.

In "Unspeakable Things Unspoken," Morrison addresses the paradox artist's face when seeking to represent traumatic experience. As she observes:

> It seemed important to me that the action in *Beloved* – the fact of infanticide – be immediately known, but deferred, unseen. I wanted to give the reader all the information and the consequences surrounding the act, while avoiding engorging myself or the reader with the violence itself. . . . I thought that the act itself had to be not only buried but also understated, because if the language was going to compete with the violence itself it would be obscene or pornographic.[16]

The passage raises important questions about the ethics of explicit description, and the appropriate discourse for articulating unspeakable suffering. It asks us to consider how an artist speaks for the suffering of those who left no or insufficient records. What discursive forms give voice to the body in pain?[17]

The figure of Beloved herself most obviously calls into question the relationship between narrative and the body. As a ghost made flesh, she is the story of the past embodied. Sethe and Denver and Paul D therefore encounter not only the story of her sorrow and theirs; they engage with its incarnation.

The very name "beloved" interrogates a number of oppositions. Simultaneously adjective and noun, the word troubles the distinction between the characteristics of a thing and the thing itself. To the extent that the title of the book is an unaccompanied modifier, it calls attention to the absence of the thing being modified. Additionally, the word "beloved" names not only the girl baby returned; in the funeral service the word addresses those who mourn the dead. The word thus names at once that which is past and present, she who is absent and those who are present.

Indeed, the word "beloved" even calls attention to the space between written and oral; until readers know the context from which her name comes, we do not know how to pronounce that name: with three syllables or two. In the terms the novel offers, Beloved might be understood to exemplify what Sethe calls "rememory," something that is past, yet remains as a physical presence.

The reader confronts the inadequacy of language perhaps most powerfully in the passages of interior monologue told from Sethe's, Denver's, and Beloved's points of view. This section follows a key moment in the novel, the point at which Stamp Paid, the man who led Sethe and her family to freedom, reveals to Paul D that Sethe murdered her daughter. (Until that point, Sethe has told Paul D that her daughter is dead, but has not told him the circumstances of her death.) Stamp Paid subsequently tries to go to Sethe's home but is kept back both by his own guilt at having told Paul D her secret, and by the "undecipherable language . . . of the black and angry dead" (p. 198). Mixed in with those voices are the thoughts of Sethe, Denver, and Beloved. In the four sections that follow, we read the unspeakable and unspoken thoughts of the three women, first separately, then interwoven. Here, from Sethe's perspective, are her memories of killing her daughter, of being beaten, of being abandoned by her mother. Largely addressed to Beloved, Sethe's words convey recollections she could never utter to another: her childhood losses, her pain at Sweet Home, the feelings that propelled her to take her child's life, and her joy at her return. Likewise, in her section, Denver expresses her fear of her mother and her yearning to be rescued by her father – anxieties that, for the most part, she had been afraid to speak.

Beloved's is the most obscure of the monologues. In it is represented the nascent subjectivity of a victim of infanticide; her richly allusive words convey the recollections and desires of someone who is at once in and out of time, alive and dead. She gives voice to her profound longing for reunion with her mother: "her face is my own and I want to be there in the place where her face is and to be looking at it too" (p. 210). But in addition to her feelings and desires from the grave, Beloved seems to have become one, in death, with those who suffered and even died during the Middle Passage, as when she describes the experience on the slave ship: "in the beginning the women are away from the men and the men are away from the women – storms rock us and mix the men into the women and the women into the men" (p. 211). In the body of Beloved, then, individual and collective pasts and memories have merged, becoming united and inseparable. The linguistic units in this section – be they sentences, phrases, or individual words – are separated by spaces, not by marks of punctuation. Only the first-person pronoun and the first letter of each paragraph are capitalized. This arrangement of words on the page places all the moments of Beloved's sensation and recollection in a continuous and eternal present.

At the end of the novel, Beloved has returned from whence she came, expelled by the prayers and exhortations of the neighbor women, and Paul D has returned to 124. In the final section of the book, she is described in terms of a series of paradoxes that seek to capture her presence within the community even though she has departed:

> Everybody knew what she was called, but nobody knew her name.

> Disremembered and unaccounted for, she cannot be lost because no one is looking for her, and even if they were, how can they call her if they don't know her name? Although she has claim, she is not claimed. (p. 274)

Twice in this chapter the phrase "It was not a story to pass on" is repeated; the third time it appears with a minor variation: "This was not a story to pass on" (pp. 274–275). As numerous critics have argued, this phrase is ambiguous. On the one hand it conveys the sense that Beloved's is a story that cannot be ignored. But it might also mean that there is danger in telling and retelling it. As Sethe, Denver, Paul D, and their neighbors have come to realize, the traumatic memories of slavery traveled with them into freedom. Their future survival depends upon their ability to face the memory of their past yet not to be consumed by its ghosts.

Notes

1 A. O. Scott, "In Search of the Best," *New York Times*, May 21, 2006. http://www.nytimes.com/2006/05/21/books/review/scott-essay.html. May 18, 2010.

2 See James Berger, "Ghosts of Liberalism: Morrison's *Beloved* and the Moynihan Report," *Publications of the Modern Language Association* 111 (May 1996): 408–420.

3 Dennis Childs, " 'You Ain't Seen Nothin' Yet:' *Beloved*, the American Chain Gang, and the Middle Passage Remix," *American Quarterly* 61 (June 2009): 271–297.

4   Critic Stanley Crouch famously took issue with the acclaim the novel received. Chief among his complaints is his sense that the novel celebrates black women's victimhood. See "Aunt Medea: *Beloved* by Toni Morrison," *The New Republic,* October 19, 1987, pp. 38–43.

5   Cheryl A. Wall, "Toni Morrison, editor and teacher," ed. Justine Tally, *The Cambridge Companion to Toni Morrison* (New York: Cambridge University Press, 2008), p. 143.

6   See Steven Weisenburger, *Modern Medea; A Family Story of Slavery and Child-Murder from the Old South* (New York: Hill and Wang, 1998). The plot of *Beloved* differs from the Margaret Garner story in that Sethe, Morrison's protagonist, left her husband for Kentucky, escaped to freedom, and was able to remain in Ohio with her living children.

7   Mervyn Rothstein, "Toni Morrison, in Her New Novel, Defends Women," *New York Times,* August 26, 1987. http://www.nytimes.com/1987/08/26/books/toni-morrison-in-her-new-novel-defends-women.html?scp=8&sq=toni+morrison+Beloved&st=ny. May 8, 2010.

8   Examples of other "neo slave narratives," as Bernard Bell calls them, or "narratives of neoslavery," the term Dennis Childs prefers, include: Arna Bontemps, *Black Thunder* (1936), Margaret Walker, *Jubilee* (1966), Gayl Jones, *Corregidora* (1975), Ishmael Reed, *Flight to Canada* (1976), Octavia Butler, *Kindred* (1979), David Bradley, *The Chaneysville Incident* (1981), Charles Johnson, *Oxherding Tale* (1982), Sherley Anne Williams, *Dessa Rose* (1986), Charles Johnson, *Middle Passage* (1990), J. California Cooper, *Family* (1991), Michelle Cliff, *Free Enterprise* (1993), Louise Meriwether, *Fragments of the Ark* (1994), Lorene Cary, *The Price of a Child* (1995), Alice Randall, *The Wind Done Gone* (2001), Edward P. Jones, *The Known World* (2003), Nancy Rawles, *My Jim* (2005), and Andrea Levy, *The Long Song* (2010). As Caroline Rody has written, "Today's most celebrated black writers, engaged in the profound mythopoetic enterprise of identification with slave ancestors, return African-American literary culture to its 'roots,' reviving with new dignity the foundational genre of this literature: the slave narrative." See her article, "Toni Morrison's *Beloved:* History, 'Rememory,' and a 'Clamor for a Kiss,'" *American Literary History* 7 (Spring 1995): p. 95. Book-length studies that focus on this genre include: Bernard Bell, *The Afro-American Novel and Its Tradition* (Amherst: University of Massachusetts Press, 1987); Ashraf H. A. Rushdy, *The Neo-Slave Narrative: Studies in the Social Logic of a Literary Form* (New York: Oxford University Press, 1999); Ashraf H. A. Rushdy, *Remembering Generations: Race and Family in Contemporary African American Fiction* (2000); Caroline Rody, *The Daughter's Return: African American and Caribbean Women's Fictions of History* (2001); Angelyn Mitchell, *The Freedom to Remember: Narrative, Slavery, and Gender*

in Contemporary Black Women's Fiction (2002); and Arlene R. Keizer, *Black Subjects: Identity Formation in the Contemporary Narrative of Slavery* (2004).

9 On this point, Karla F. C. Holloway has written: "The victim's own chronicles of these events were systematically submerged, ignored, mistrusted, or superseded by 'historians' of the era. This novel positions the consequences of black invisibility in both the records of slavery and the record-keeping as a situation of primary spiritual significance." See "*Beloved:* A Spiritual," in *Beloved: A Casebook,* ed. William L. Andrews and Nellie Y. McKay (New York: Oxford University Press, 1999), p. 68.

10 Toni Morrison, "The Site of Memory," in ed. William Zinsser, *Inventing the Truth: The Art and Craft of Memoir* (Boston, MA: Houghton Mifflin, 1987a), p. 112.

11 Toni Morrison, *Beloved* (New York: Knopf, 1987b), p. 36. Subsequent references will be cited parenthetically in the text.

12 Morrison, "The Art of Fiction CXXXIV," *The Paris Review* 128 (Fall 1993): 103.

13 See Morrison's eloquent analysis of the opening sentences of *Beloved* in her essay, "Unspeakable Things Unspoken: The Afro-American Presence in American Literature," *Michigan Quarterly Review* 28.1 (Winter 1989): 31–32.

14 As Linda Krumholz has written, Schoolteacher is the "moral absolute of evil" in the novel. His pedagogical methods embody "politically motivated versions of history while masking those representations in a rhetoric of 'facts' and scientific method." See her article, "The Ghosts of Slavery: Historical Recovery in Toni Morrison's *Beloved,*" *African American Review* 26 (Autumn 1992): 398–399.

15 "Sixty Million and More" is the phrase Morrison uses in the dedication to *Beloved.* For an analysis of the debate this phrase occasioned, see Naomi Mandel, "'I Made the Ink:' Identity, Complicity, 60 Million, and More," *Modern Fiction Studies* 48.3 (Fall 2002): 581–613.

16 Morrison, "The Art of Fiction CXXXIV," pp. 110–111.

17 For examples of critical and theoretical texts that address this issue, see: Elaine Scarry, *The Body in Pain: The Making and Unmaking of the World* (New York: Oxford University Press, 1985); Dominick LaCapra, *Writing History, Writing Trauma* (Baltimore, MD: Johns Hopkins University Press, 2001); and Jacqueline D. Goldsby, *A Spectacular Secret: Lynching in American Life and Literature* (Chicago, IL: University of Chicago Press, 2006).

CHAPTER 4

Jazz and *Paradise*

Jazz

Between 1982 and 1997, Toni Morrison published three novels to which she and many of her critics have referred collectively as a trilogy: *Beloved* (1987), *Jazz* (1992), and *Paradise* (1998). These novels are considered a trilogy for a variety of reasons. Some critics have argued that they are connected by their shared focus on the relationship between excessive love and violence: *Beloved* on maternal love, *Jazz* on romantic love, and *Paradise* on religious or communal love. They have been called a trilogy because of their historical reach: read chronologically, the novels span 100 years of African American life and cover a broad geographic area. *Beloved* is set during the 1870s outside Cincinnati, Ohio with flashbacks to a plantation in Kentucky and a chain gang in Alfred, Georgia. *Jazz* is set in 1920s Harlem with flashbacks to Reconstruction era Virginia. *Paradise* is set mostly in the 1970s in the all-black town of Ruby, Oklahoma, but the text is flooded with memories of the ancestors, the "Old Fathers" who left Louisiana and Mississippi and founded Haven in the 1870s after the failure of Reconstruction. All three novels are set against the backdrop of a war – the Civil War, World War I, the Vietnam War. Perhaps most significantly, all three offer revisions of critical periods in US history

Toni Morrison: Writing the Moral Imagination, First Edition. Valerie Smith.
© 2012 Valerie Smith. Published 2014 by John Wiley & Sons, Ltd.

by foregrounding the underacknowledged experiences of African Americans.[1]

Just as the plot of *Beloved* grew out of a news item of which Morrison became aware when she was compiling *The Black Book*, the plot of *Jazz* was inspired by a photograph Morrison encountered while she was preparing the Foreword to a collection of images shot by the legendary African American photographer James Van Der Zee entitled *The Harlem Book of the Dead*.[2] As Van Der Zee tells Camille Billops in an interview included in *The Harlem Book of the Dead*:

> [The girl in the photograph] was shot by her sweetheart at a party with a noiseless gun. She complained of being sick at the party and friends said, 'Well, why don't you lay down?' and they taken her in the room and laid her down. After they undressed her and loosened her clothes, they saw the blood on her dress. They asked her about it and she said, 'I'll tell you tomorrow, yes, I'll tell you tomorrow.' She was just trying to give him a chance to get away. For the picture, I placed the flowers on her chest.[3]

For Morrison, the young woman's self-destructive desire to protect her vengeful lover seemed "redolent of the proud hopelessness of love mourned and championed in blues music, and, simultaneously, fired by the irresistible energy of jazz music" (p. xvi).[4]

The plot of *Jazz* is essentially summarized in its first pages. In the opening lines of the novel, we read of a woman named Violet whose husband murdered the 18-year-old girl named Dorcas with whom he was having an affair. At the young woman's funeral, Violet tried to slash the dead girl's face as she lay in her coffin, and the ushers ejected her; upon her return home, she released her pet birds from the windows, "to freeze or fly" (p. 3). But *Jazz* is about much more than these events. Like *The Bluest Eye, Sula, Song of Solomon,* and *Tar Baby,* it is concerned with the impact of migration from the south to the north upon African American individuals and communities. As *Beloved* revised conventional understandings of the period of slavery, *Jazz* revises received ideas about African American migration. Moreover, the novel explores the role of jazz music in the lives of the characters and the community in which they live. The sound and the form of jazz, a musical genre that constituted at least part of soundtrack of the urban streetscape of Harlem in the early decades of the twentieth century, inform the narrative voice. Not only does the sound of jazz infuse the characters' inner lives and leisure activities, but it shapes the aesthetic of the novel as well. In her experimentation with narrative voice, Morrison interrogates prevailing notions about the Jazz Age and demonstrates the complexity and multifariousness of African American lives in the north.

Perhaps even more keenly than in her earlier novels, in *Jazz* Morrison suggests that for African American migrants from the south in the first half of the twentieth century, the move north proved to be a mixed blessing. Traditionally, migration northward has been understood as a means by which African Americans escaped the most virulent forms of racial oppression in the south and found opportunities for economic, political, and educational advancement. In this instance, Violet, Joe, and the other migrants in the novel – both named and unnamed – are propelled northward because of the personal losses and economic and political injustices they experienced both directly and indirectly. They are captivated by all the City has to offer, but as the novel unfolds, it reveals the effects of their separation from community, the land, and their families.

As the narrator observes, the African American migrants left behind not only political and economic exploitation; they left behind the image of their own and their people's subservience as well. Up North, they discover their autonomy, "the New Negroes" around and within themselves.[5] However humble their living conditions in the City:

> they stayed to look at their number, hear themselves moving down the street among hundreds of others who moved the way they did, and who, when they spoke, regardless of the accent, treated language like the same intricate, malleable toy designed for their play. (pp. 32–33)

Yet as they are seduced by the energy, the architecture, and the culture of the City, they also become consumed by their own desires, objectifying other people instead of loving them, and becoming objectified themselves.

When Alice Manfred, Dorcas's aunt, leaves Illinois (first for Springfield, Massachusetts and then for New York), she hopes that she has left behind the sexual threat of white men and her parents' protective yet obsessive preoccupation with her body and her sexuality.[6] But while she may be able to leave home, she cannot leave behind her their hypervigilance and the historic oppression of black women from which it springs. Not only does her husband abandon her, but she finds as well that up north, white men and women alike continue to see her body as debased and oversexed. Eventually, she realizes that anywhere south of Harlem she feels less than human. When the young Dorcas comes to live with her, Alice recognizes how fully she has internalized the system she had hoped to escape. Doomed to recapitulate her parents' oppressive behavior, she polices her niece's body and sexuality in much the same way that her parents policed hers.

Dorcas moves to the City to live with her Aunt Alice after her parents are killed during the East St. Louis, Illinois riots of 1917.[7] One of many literally or figuratively orphaned characters in the novel, she has sustained a familial loss that anticipates the cultural loss she experiences when she leaves home for the City. The deaths of her parents and the ensuing geographical displacement undermine her understanding of who she is. This sense of self-alienation is inscribed upon her body and in her features. She is a young woman whose clothing is never quite right; the conservative outfits her aunt forces her to wear fail to constrain the bodily assertiveness that comes with adolescent girlhood. Later on, when she and her best friend Felice sneak out to go to a party, she has the opposite problem. Despite their best efforts, her clothing cannot be made to seem festive or alluring.

Out of sync with her age, her body, and her identity, Dorcas enters into an affair with Joe, a man old enough to be her father, and then rejects him 3 months later for Acton, a man her own age. Joe worships Dorcas – flaws, idiosyncrasies and all – but his love is insufficient for her. She may sense that he loves her for reasons that have nothing to do with her; as he realizes after her murder, in her, at least for a moment, he is able to satisfy in his longing for his lost mother.[8] She also feels that her relationship with Joe is inadequate because it lacks value as a commodity. No one knows about them both because of Joe's marital status and because of the difference in their ages; their affair thus has no value as a spectacle and thus lacks value for her. Moreover, in her relationship with Joe, she feels as if she does not quite exist. Because Joe loves her as she is, she cannot find a way to see herself in his eyes. In contrast, as a handsome man her own age, Acton has a higher commodity value; with him, Dorcas is able to enjoy a relationship that others regard with envy.

When she thinks about Acton, the erotic energy of her enthusiasm is palpable; her language is replete with references to desire, ownership, and objectification. She wants to have Acton, to have friends talk about their relationship, about "things" and "stuff:"

> I had this chance to have Acton and I wanted it and I wanted girlfriends to talk about it. About where we went and what we did. About things. About stuff. What good are secrets if you can't talk to anybody about them? (p. 189)

Moreover, when Acton criticizes her appearance and appetite, he unknowingly helps her define herself in relation to prevailing norms of women's beauty and sex appeal. As she puts it, her personality is located and expressed in her ability to conform to the latest styles:

> I wanted to have a personality and with Acton I'm getting one. I have a look now. What pencil-thin eyebrows do for my face is a dream. All my bracelets are just below my elbow. Sometimes I knot my stockings below, not above, my knees. Three straps are across my instep and at home I have shoes with leather cut out to look like lace. (p. 190)

Joe and Violet left Tyrell, Vesper County, Virginia in 1906, ostensibly out of frustration with the exploitative economic conditions under which they labored; like many African Americans in the Jim Crow south, they had been cheated by the farmer whose land they share-cropped. The idea of the City seduces them with its power; they identify with and anthropomorphize the rhythm of the rocking northbound train. Joe and Violet easily find work in the City and enjoy their new-found prosperity. However, with time and distance away from home, they begin to deteriorate psychologically and spiritually as they confront the deep losses they sustained in their childhood and youth. As Angelyn Mitchell has shown, Violet is descended from a line of women who suffered from the political, economic, and personal traumas of the eras of slavery and Reconstruction.[9] With no regard for her own desires or relationships, True Belle, her grandmother, was snatched away from her own family and sent to live in Baltimore with her young mistress, Vera Louise, once Vera Louise's parents discovered she was pregnant by the black man with whom she used to ride horses. True Belle grew to love Golden Gray, Vera Louise's child, but that love stemmed at least in part from her love of his pale skin and long curly hair, and it gradually helped her adjust to the separation from her own family.

Rose Dear, Violet's mother, was left to raise her children by herself when her husband was chased out of town because of his political activities and affiliations. With no visible means of support, she is unable to prevent her creditors from removing her possessions. When Rose Dear and her children are on the brink of utter ruin, a neighbor summons True Belle who returns and stays 11 years to care for her family. But 4 years after her mother's arrival, Rose Dear takes her own life by throwing herself down a well. Witness to her own mother's deterioration, Violet vows never to be a mother herself. By the time of the narrative present, Violet's own disintegration has begun. On one occasion, she simply stops and sits down in the middle of the street; another time, she attempts to kidnap a child. Moreover, as she begins to feel her identity splitting apart, she experiences herself as two discrete persons. Once a "snappy, determined girl and a hard-working young woman," by the period when the novel begins, she perceives her own actions as a series of "small, well-lit scenes," but does not realize that she is the person responsible for them (pp. 22–23). Her self-alienation causes her to withdraw from Joe as well; in response to her fears that she is losing him, she overeats compulsively in a vain attempt to grow larger hips and make herself more desirable. Living in the City feeds her desire to escape herself and become someone else. As Mitchell observes, Violet has more freedom of choice than her grandmother and more economic power than her mother, but she is alienated from herself in the urban north. As Mitchell writes: "Violet attempts to mediate her private rural self with her public urban self, her motherless rural self with her daughterless urban self."[10]

Joe is the son of an unknown father and a mother called Wild who is more at home in the wilderness than she is in the company of other people. Abandoned as a child, he was raised by Rhoda and Frank

Williams as one of their own. Before Dorcas, the only person in whom he could confide his deepest feelings is Victory, Rhoda's and Frank's son and his closest friend. His passion for Dorcas is fueled by more than simply his lust for a young, attractive woman. With her, he perceives an opportunity to revisit and restage pivotal moments in his past. For example, when he first meets Violet, he falls out of a tree and lands by her side one night as she prepares to fall asleep. By the following morning, she has claimed him and he willingly goes along with her. As he recalls: "he had not chosen that but was grateful, in fact, that he didn't have to; that Violet did it for him, helping him escape all the redwings in the county and the ripe silence that accompanied them" (p. 30). In contrast, when he sees Dorcas, she awakens a desire in him he has never known. He loves both her and the version of himself that possesses sufficient power and agency to pursue her.

Besides allowing Joe to revisit and revise his initial encounter with Violet, Dorcas also reconnects him with his feelings of loss for his mother. Violet's retreat from their marriage conjures up that loss. In Dorcas he believes he has found someone who can share the orphan's feeling of abandonment. When she leaves him for Acton, he hunts her down not only out of jealousy and possession, but also as a way of re-staging his search for his mother.

In her "Foreword," Morrison firmly situates the novel in the 1920s, the period that has come to be known as the Jazz Age. While jazz and African American culture are commonly portrayed as ancillary to the energy and excess associated with post-World War I economic growth and social, cultural and dynamism, they are the central focus of this novel.[11] Some of Morrison's most evocative writing describes the ways in which jazz infuses the characters' lives. It can be found in the description of Joe's and Violet's bodies swaying and rocking to the movement of the train that carries them into New York for the first time (p. 32). Despite her fear and disapproval, the music captivates Alice Manfred because it captures the synergy between political and sexual awareness. She may have been raised to avoid secular music, but she cannot deny its urgent rhythms.

Moreover, in this novel Morrison finds the space where prose and music intersect; jazz infuses the rhythm, timbre, and flow of the narrative voice. For instance, in this description of the signs one might encounter on a Harlem street, marks of punctuation gradually disappear and parts of speech begin to shift:

> The City is smart at this: smelling and good and looking raunchy; sending secret messages disguised as public signs: this way, open here, danger to let colored only single men on sale woman wanted private room stop dog on premises absolutely no money down fresh chicken free delivery fast. (p. 64)

The passage requires the reader to slow down, re-read, to give oneself over to the rhythm of the words. In the process of surrender, multiple significations begin to emerge. The public signs lose their more generic meaning and point to the sexual threat that single "colored" men and women pose for each other in the commodified space of the city.

Similarly, Morrison captures Dorcas's and her friend Felice's fascination with the music and the sexual tension they encounter at a party in her description of a pause between dances, where young men and women collect themselves. Here, in the break, time is suspended, nouns become verbs and vice versa, and the reader is forced to pause and imagine the moist, hot air the room of bodies has generated:

> In between record changes, while the girls fan blouse necks to air damp collarbones or pat with anxious hands the damage moisture has done to their hair, the boys press folded handkerchiefs to their foreheads. (p. 65)

Jazz represents one of Morrison's boldest narrative experiments. From the opening sentence, one questions the identity of the narrator: "Sth, I know that woman" (p. 3).[12] The easy, off-the-cuff, vernacular familiarity, suggest that the narrator might be a neighbor. Moreover, as Morrison has observed, the unnamed narrator functions as a musician whose opening paragraph provides the melody. Throughout the course of the novel, the characters – Malvonne, Alice, Violet, Joe, Dorcas, and Felice – offer up solos that elaborate and improvise upon the basic story. By the end of the book, when Joe and Violet have befriended Felice and created a quasi-family unit with her, the reader understands that the ensemble has created a version of the story that is more complex than the summary with which the text opens. Indeed, even the narrator herself recognizes that her version oversimplifies her characters' lives.[13]

At the same time, Morrison also invites us to understand the narrator to be the novel itself:

> *Jazz* was very complicated because I wanted to re-present two contradictory things – artifice and improvisation, where you have an artwork, planned, thought through, but at the same time appears invented, like jazz. I thought of the image being a book. Physically a book, but at the same time it is writing itself. Imagining itself. Talking. Aware of what it is doing. It watches itself think and imagine. That seemed to me to be a combination of artifice and improvisation – where you practice and plan in order to invent. . . . *Jazz* predicts its own story. Sometimes it is wrong because of faulty vision. It simply did not imagine those characters well enough, admit it was wrong, and the characters talk back the way jazz musicians do. It has to listen to the characters it has invented, and then learn something from them. It was the most intricate thing I had done, though I wanted to tell a very simple story about people who do not know that they are living in the Jazz age, and to never use the word.[14]

And indeed, the narrator does mislead the reader and feel the need to apologize for her erroneous assertions about characters and their motivations.

To the extent that Morrison explores the period known as the Jazz Age from the perspective of the excess of desire and romantic love, the book itself signifies the nexus of the relationship between music, narrative, and intimacy. In the first chapter, the narrator reflects upon the feeling of being ignored by one's partner, and that partner might as easily be a lover as a reader:

> I lived a long time, maybe too much, in my own mind. People say I should come out more. Mix. I agree that I close off in places, but if you have been left standing, as I have, while your partner overstays at another appointment, or promises to give you exclusive attention after supper, but is falling asleep just as you have begun to speak – well, it can make you inhospitable if you aren't careful, the last thing I want to be. (p. 9)

Likewise, the lines with which the novel ends might be construed either as yearning for a lost love, or an invitation into the intimacy of the reading relationship:

I love the way you hold me, how close you let me be to you. I like your fingers on and on, lifting, turning. I have watched your face for a long time now, and missed your eyes when you went away from me. Talking to you and hearing your answer – that's the kick.

But I can't say that aloud; I can't tell anyone that I have been waiting for this all my life and that being chosen to wait is the reason I can. If I were able I'd say it. Say make me, remake me. You are free to do it and I am free to let you because look, look. Look where your hands are. Now. (p. 229)

Paradise

In the Judeo-Christian tradition, Paradise is another name for the Garden of Eden, where God's first creations resided until their fall from grace. The title of Morrison's seventh novel invokes that ideal world and the myth of origins it contains, deploying it as a metaphor for the quest to create and maintain a protected, homogeneous world. Morrison's Paradise is the all-black town of Ruby, Oklahoma, where the novel is primarily set. Established by a core group of men and their families in 1949, it recalls a number of all-black towns formed during the Jim Crow era to consolidate African American resources and protect their residents from the threat of white violence. Few of these all-black towns remain, but they are often recalled nostalgically as places where black people worked in harmony for the common good.

In *Paradise* Morrison grapples with the implications of one question in particular: why do our notions of utopia depend upon separation and exclusion? Why is the idea of paradise as much about those we include as it is about those we keep out? Ruby, Oklahoma descended from the town of Haven, which was founded by the patriarchs of nine black families who led more than a hundred formerly enslaved black people from Louisiana and Mississippi to the Oklahoma Territory after they were expelled from positions of power – generally in government – in the years following Reconstruction. By 1889, several such all-black towns had been established in the Oklahoma Territory, and these towns advertised for settlers. But the eager, dark-skinned black folks known as "8-Rock" who eventually settled Haven, soon discovered that the other towns were inhabited by light-skinned blacks who wanted nothing to do with them.[15] As the narrator observes:

Oh, they knew there was a difference in the minds of whites, but it had not struck them before that it was of consequence, serious consequence, to Negroes themselves. Serious enough that their daughters would be shunned as brides; their sons chosen last; that colored men would be embarrassed to be seen socially with their sisters. The sign of racial purity they had taken for granted had become a stain. (p. 194)

The founders of Haven prayed for a Paradise where they could shield themselves from further rejection. For a time, Haven was just that sort of utopia. But by the end of World War II, that first town had fallen into decline. The generation of veterans decided to migrate westward yet again and start another Paradise, the town that came to be called Ruby. The new generation of founding fathers was so fiercely protective and fully enamored of the story of their ancestors, that they determined to replicate the spirit of Haven in the new town. It was to be founded on the same principles upon which Haven had been built in the nineteenth century. It was to be a strongly patriarchal community, closed to outsiders and outside influences, and devoted to preserving the memory of the ancestors. The townspeople were committed to the notion that their residents should marry only other 8-Rock families; they shunned any man who married a woman from outside their community, especially if she were light-skinned.

On the surface, certain aspects of the life of the town are admirable. There is no crime; people are self-sufficient, and no one seems to die there. But the town is clearly in decline; it is haunted by the specter of infertility and thwarted procreation. By virtue of their wealth and the force of their character, twins Deacon and Steward Morgan are town leaders, yet Steward and his wife Dovey are infertile and Deacon and his wife Soane (Dovey's sister) lost both of their sons to the Vietnam War. Nathan DuPres and his wife Mirth lost all of their children in a tornado that hit Haven in 1922. And Jeff and Sweetie Fleetwood have four bedridden children, all suffering from severe disabilities. Moreover, the very homogeneity and insularity in which they pride themselves carry the seeds of the town's dissolution. The town leaders want nothing to do with black political activism, whether in the form of the Civil Rights Movement or Black Nationalist politics, or an African diasporic consciousness. As a result, they can find no common ground with the younger generation who seek to find a place for such activism in their community.

The central symbol of Haven, the earlier town, was a communal oven that bore an iron plate that purportedly read: "Beware the Furrow of His Brow." This oven was the first thing the Old Fathers built when they settled in Haven.

> [It both] nourished them and monumentalized what they had done. When it was finished – each pale brick perfectly pitched; the chimney wide, lofty; the pegs and grill secure; the draft pulling steadily from the tail hole; the fire door plumb – then the ironmonger did his work. From barrel staves and busted axles, from kettles and bent nails, he fashioned an iron plate five feet by two and set it at the base of the Oven's mouth. It is still not clear where the words came from. Something he heard, invented, or something whispered to him while he slept curled over his tools in a wagon bed. . . . Words that seemed at first to bless them; later to confound them, finally to announce that they had lost. (p. 7)

When the townspeople relocated, they lovingly dismantled the oven, moved it with them, and continued to worship it even after they could all afford, and in fact used, the ovens in their own homes. In the narrative present, the 1970s, the new generation of younger people want to use the oven in the town square as a place where they can congregate, socialize, and engage in political organization. They even venture to reinterpret the words on the oven. When they scrutinize the faded lettering, they believe that it reads: "Be the Furrow of His Brow." The struggle around the language and the function of the oven itself pits two visions of history against each other. The elder generation clings to a static view of history, where meanings are rigid and codified; the younger seeks a usable past that can be shaped and mobilized to serve the needs of the present. The conflict around the use of the oven and the words inscribed upon it encapsulates the competing visions of history that lie at the heart of the novel.

The story of Ruby provides the occasion for a critique of exclusionary practices of patriarchy, race, and misogyny. References to Christian institutions as well as Biblical narratives and characters pervade the history and rituals of the community and help the residents justify their faith in their own exceptionalism. For instance, the Morgan family, the town's first family (as determined by wealth and the force of personality) is descended from the union of Zechariah and his wife Mindy. As Patricia Best, a teacher and the town's informal genealogist observes, the names of the sons, Pryor, Rector, Shepherd, Governor, and Scout are all "administrative, authoritative-sounding"(p. 191). The names of Rector's twin sons, Deacon and Steward, who dominate the town in the narrative present, invoke positions of leadership within Protestant denominations. Moreover, the town commemorates its founding in an annual pageant that essentially recasts the Nativity. In their ritual re-enactment of the Disallowing – their name for the ancestors' experience of being rejected by other all-black towns – the original families are constructed as a collection of Josephs and Marys, their offspring as Christ-figures. These convergences of religion and history are but two examples that signal the townspeople's excessive and sanctimonious investment in their own mythmaking.

In its representation of the uses to which the townspeople put Christianity, the novel points to the ways in which a community forged in opposition to the exclusionary practices of a dominant culture replicates and legitimates its own exclusionary practices. If the national myth of American exceptionalism and belief in its origins in a city on a hill depends upon the exploitation of black, brown, and native peoples, *Paradise* explores how analogous myths of the sacredness of their origins both underlie and legitimate Ruby's own racial hierarchies. As Lucille P. Fultz and others have noted, even more specifically, the novel invites us to consider the town of Ruby in relation to the New England Puritans. Like the Puritans, the founders of Haven and Ruby "see their mission as a divine calling to establish an inviolate and inviolable . . . community."[16] When those norms are violated, they find it all too easy to scapegoat women they brand as outlaws, even going so far as to call them witches.

Indeed, at its core, the novel is preoccupied with stories of origins. The descendants of the Founding Fathers are so fully enthralled by the memory of their ancestors that they can think of no better tribute than to recapitulate that past as literally as possible. They consider any alternative to that historical construct to be a threat, and they seek to challenge it. That threat takes the form of the younger generation, who seek to find a place for themselves and the town within the Civil Rights and Black Nationalist struggles that loom so large in the outside world. And it takes the form of anyone – especially women – who threaten the racial purity of their community.

The novel thus critiques the convergence of religion and history within the town itself, and it establishes an alternative formation in the Convent, a community of women located 17 miles outside of Ruby.

Originally a mansion built by a gambler, earlier in the twentieth century, nuns converted it into the Christ the King School for Indian Girls. In 1949, the Convent, as it came to be known, was running out of funding and subjects for its mission. By 1968, only Consolata, kidnapped as a child from Brazil, and the nun who stole her away, remained. In that year, the Convent assumed a new mission: sheltering women who had been abused, jilted, rejected, or outcast; all women who had lost their way and had nowhere else to go. While Ruby is patriarchal, the Convent is matriarchal. While Ruby is a homogeneous community organized around racial purity, the Convent is heterogeneous. We know that at least one white woman lives there, and yet Morrison never identifies the women by race.

The novel turns on what Ruby's patriarchs decide are the first signs that their Paradise is threatened. The youth have caught the fever of the 1960s and want the town to change. The women of the town begin to forge relationships with Convent women. Convinced that the Convent women – Consolata, Mavis, Gigi, Seneca, and Pallas – are the source of the problems that they believe will threaten the integrity of their town, nine men from Ruby ride out there to eliminate them. Here is where the novel begins; the meandering plot explains who the victims and perpetrators are and explores the motives behind the desire to massacre the women.

This overview might suggest that the plot of the novel is fairly straightforward. In fact, the plot is anything but that. In March 1998, the novel was the focus of the thirteenth Book Club episode of the Oprah Winfrey show.[17] Winfrey's readers found the novel to be so difficult that Winfrey decided to alter the format of the show. Typically, in the Book Club episodes, readers would discuss their personal responses to and identification with the featured novel; they sit in comfortably appointed rooms, sip wine, and talk. When *Paradise* was the featured novel, however, the discussion took place in a classroom at Princeton University, and Morrison herself led the conversation.[18]

These readers' difficulty with the novel was not merely a function of their expectations derived from the types of books typically selected for the Club. Even experienced readers of Morrison's fiction will find it especially challenging for a variety of reasons. As is the case in several of her novels – *Beloved*, *Jazz*, and *Love*, for example, the novel lacks a linear plot. In those other cases, with a bit of work the reader is able to puzzle out the sequence of events. But while reading *Paradise*, it is much harder to locate oneself in a given historical moment. The narrative present seems to be 1976. At some times in the novel we find ourselves in 1948, at others in 1968, in yet others in 1973 or 1974. We might find ourselves at one moment in time in one chapter or page or paragraph, and in another in the next chapter or page or paragraph.

Like *The Bluest Eye*, *Sula*, *Jazz*, and *Love*, the novel begins with its ending. Before we know anything about either the perpetrators or the victims, we read in the opening paragraph that the women at the Convent have been targeted for violence:

> They shoot the white girl first. With the rest they can take their time. No need to hurry out here. They are seventeen miles from a town which has ninety miles between it and any other. Hiding places will be plentiful in the Convent, but there is time and the day has just begun. (p. 3)

That opening sentence is something of a tease. It tempts the reader into thinking that we can use the racial detail to orient ourselves in the plot. But Morrison never identifies the women by race. Her refusal to rely on racial markers makes readers aware of the ways in which we use – indeed overuse – these tropes as we read texts and as we read people. Here, as in her short story entitled "Recitatif" (1983), she asks us to consider what it would mean to encounter each other without the props of racial cues and stereotypes.[19] In this regard, the novel speaks back to or undercuts the townspeople's preoccupation with racial purity. Its very refusal to submit to the protocols of racial representation challenges the ontological basis of the town of Ruby. Indeed, Morrison emphasizes the socioeconomic racial and ethnic multiplicity of the Convent by housing black women from different regions of the country, Consolata from Brazil, and one white woman in a school that was originally intended for Native American women.

Furthermore, the novel challenges readers by featuring a strikingly large number of characters – most with unusual names – whose lives cross either accidentally, or whose lives are intricately connected. Each has a story; it can be confusing to keep these various narratives straight and figure out how they link to one another. The narrative present takes place in the 1970s, but many of the characters are bound to fantasy lives that stretch back several generations. And the novel takes place in isolated communities – the all-black town of Ruby, Oklahoma and a former convent inhabited by a group of lost and victimized women on the outskirts of town. Both locations are shaped by their own rules and cut off from the influence of the outside world.

Morrison herself has said that all of these elements are designed to re-create for the reader the experience of entering a new environment and gradually getting to know it through the accumulation of partial knowledge. Timothy Aubry takes this point one step further, and rightly observes that Morrison "insists on a challenging form of social and psychological inclusivity, an openness to unfamiliar experiences, modes of discourse, concepts, and identities seemingly at odds with the restrictive gatekeeping measures typically at work in conventional versions of paradise."[20] In other words, the reading experience itself demands an expansiveness antithetical to the sort of self-protectiveness that typically underwrites ideas of paradise and the assumptions upon which Ruby is built.

While I share Aubry's view, I also believe that two of the narrative projects within the text shed light upon the challenges it poses. The first is Patricia Best's genealogical project. An elementary school teacher, Patricia is at work on a local history of Ruby. Originally meant to be a gift to the townspeople, the history was intended to map out the genealogies of the town's 15 leading families. But as she sought to document information gleaned from oral histories and anecdotes, she found that the townspeople grew suspicious, then reticent. Finally, she realized that the project was more interesting and valuable to her than it was to her neighbors, and that it interested her for reasons other than her initial motivation; it began to suggest an alternative to the patriarchal logic upon which the town had depended for generations:

> The project became unfit for any eyes except her own. It had reached the point where the small *m* period was a joke; a dream, a violation of law that had her biting her thumbnail in frustration. Who were those women who, like her mother, had only one name? Celeste, Olive, Sorrow, Ivlin, Pansy. Who were these women with generalized last names? Brown, Smith, Rivers, Stone, Jones. Women whose identity rested on the men they married – if marriage applied a Morgan, a Flood, a Blackhorse, a Poole, a Fleetwood. (pp. 187–188)

Pat's frustration with trying to keep names, dates, and relationships straight mirrors our own in the process of reading. At some point she realizes that the story lies in the "footnotes, crevices, questions" (p. 188) and silences that the linearity of patriarchal genealogy eschews, indeed fears. And she realizes that her narrative must account for the women, like her own mother, who have been erased from or subordinated within dominant narrative accounts.[21] At the end of the chapter that bears her name, she burns her notes. She recognizes, as perhaps we must, the limits of getting lost in the details. In working hard enough to assemble data one can gather certain truths. But the facts can take us only so far, and it is in the shared experience as well as the interplay between details and ellipses that we can find history and community.

We see that vision enacted even more powerfully at the Convent itself. The Convent women begin their lives together in contention, jockeying for power, attention, and affection, but they grow into community through the process of shared narration – "loud dreaming" (p. 264) – in which Consolata leads them. In the "loud dreaming," each woman gets to share her own story of trauma. Guided by Consolata, each paints images of her suffering, is able to see that suffering for what it is, and comes to understand the connections between and among their own experiences. Moreover, in the "loud dreaming" they learn to listen actively and inhabit each other's suffering. In the end, it is this band of outlaw women at the Convent who may provide a deeper sense of community than that which the patriarchs seek so aggressively to enforce.

The scene of "loud dreaming" reveals the process by which these women, all victims of abuse, find healing and community. From the perspective of the town patriarchs, however, the existence of this house of women, unprotected and undisciplined by men, constitutes a threat to the values they cherish. Steward Morgan justifies the attack on the Convent women when he observes:

> The women of the Convent were for him a flaunting parody of the nineteen Negro Ladies of his and his brother's youthful memory and perfect understanding. They were the degradation of that moment they'd shared of sunlit skin and verbena . . . he could not abide them for sullying his personal history with their streetwalkers' clothes and whores' appetites. (p. 279)

In the final section, "Save-Marie," we learn from Pat's perspective that not only are there multiple explanations of what happened on the day of the attack and multiple interpretations of who is to blame, but that in the absence of the women's bodies, it is unclear which ones and how many of them have died. It should thus not surprise us that a novel in which the living and the dead communicate and characters are resurrected, Gigi, Pallas, Mavis, and Seneca – all women whom we might have assumed to have been slaughtered – seem to reappear in the lives of those they had loved in their earlier lives. Each woman disappears after meeting her lost friend or relative, leaving both the reader and her lost loved one uncertain as to whether the encounter actually occurred. As Lucille P. Fultz argues, this ending is an image of their "apotheosis or transubstantiation," a re-claiming of the meaning of Christ's resurrection.[22]

Notes

1   For discussions of the trilogy, see Louis Menand, "The War between Men and Women," review of *Paradise, The New Yorker,* January 12, 1998, pp. 78–82; Barbara Christian, " 'The Past is Infinite': History and Myth in Toni Morrison's Trilogy," *Social Identities* 6.4 (2000): 411–423; and Justine Tally, "The Morrison Trilogy," in *The Cambridge Companion to Toni Morrison,* ed. Justine Tally, (New York: Cambridge University Press, 2007), pp. 75–91.

2   This collection combines Van Der Zee's photographs with poetic text by Owen Dodson and Van Der Zee's extended interview with Camille Billops. The photograph that inspired *Jazz* features an elaborately dressed young woman lying in repose in a bier surrounded by flowers. Superimposed in the top left-hand corner is an image of Jesus Christ looking on her. On the facing page we find these lines from poet Owen Dodson:

> *They lean over me and say:*
> *'Who deathbed you who,*
> *who, who, who, who. . . .'*
> *I whisper: 'Tell you presently . . .*
> *Shortly . . . this evening. . . .*
> *Tomorrow . . .'*
> *Tomorrow is here*
> *And you out there safe.*
> *I'm safe in here, Tootsie.*

See James Van Der Zee, Owen Dodson, Camille Billops, *The Harlem Book of the Dead* (Dobbs Ferry, NY: Morgan and Morgan, 1978), pp. 52–53.

3   *Harlem Book of the Dead*, p. 84.

4   Toni Morrison, *Jazz* (New York: Knopf, 1992a), p. xvi. Subsequent references will be to this edition.

5   See Michelle Stephens, "The Harlem Renaissance: The New Negro at Home and Abroad," in *A Companion to African American Literature*, ed. Gene Andrew Jarrett (Oxford: Wiley-Blackwell, 2010), pp. 212–226.

6   During her adolescence they worry that her every gesture invites male attention. Once she marries they fret over her younger sisters' sexuality and push her to have children. See pp. 76–77.

7   The East St. Louis Riots of May and July 1917 rank among the deadliest incidents of racially-motivated and labor-related violence in twentieth-century US culture. On July 28, 1917, 10,000 people marched down Fifth Avenue in New York City in a silent protest of the East St. Louis riots organized by the National Association for the Advancement of Colored People. See Elliott Rudwick, *Race Riot at East St. Louis: July 2, 1917* (Carbondale: Southern Illinois University Press, 1964; rpt. Urbana: University Press of Illinois, 1982).

8   As Evelyn Jaffe Schreiber rightly notes, Joe seeks not only his mother, but also "the ability to verbalize his trauma in order to name his own desire." See Evelyn Jaffe Schreiber, *Race, Trauma, and Home in the Novels of Toni Morrison* (Baton Rouge, LA: Louisiana state University Press, 2010), p. 114.

9   See Angelyn Mitchell, "'Sth, I Know that Woman': History, Gender, and the South in Toni Morrison's *Jazz*," *Studies in the Literary Imagination* 31.2 (Fall 1998): 49–60. She argues that True Belle may be read in relation to the gendered history of slavery, Rose Dear in relation to the gendered history of Reconstruction, and Violet to the gendered history of the Great Migration.

10   Mitchell, p. 57.

11   Scholars have increasingly explored the rich ways in which modernism shaped and was shaped by constructions of race. See, for example, Houston A. Baker, *Modernism and the Harlem Renaissance* (Chicago: University of Chicago Press, 1989); Ann Douglas, *Terrible Honesty: Mongrel Manhattan in the 1920s* (New York: Farrar, Straus and Giroux, 1995); Michael North, *The Dialect of Modernism: Race, Language, and Twentieth Century Literature* (New York: Oxford University Press, 1998).

12   Numerous critics have written about the identity of the narrator. See, for example, Philip Page, "Traces of Derrida in Toni Morrison's *Jazz*," *African American Review* 29.1 (Spring 1995): 55–66; Veronique Lesoinne, "Answer Jazz's Call: Experiencing Toni Morrison's *Jazz*," *Multi-Ethnic*

Literature of the U.S. 22.3 (Autumn 1997): 151–166; Caroline Rody, "Impossible Voices: Ethnic Postmodern Narration in Toni Morrison's *Jazz* and Karen Tei Yamashita's *Through the Arc of the Rain Forest*," *Contemporary Literature* 41.4 (2000): 618–641; Caroline Brown, "Golden Gray and the Talking Book: Identity as a Site of Artful Construction in Toni Morrison's *Jazz*," *African American Review* 36.4 (Winter 2002): 629–642; Matthew Treherne, "Figuring In, Figuring Out: Narration and Negotiation in Toni Morrrison's *Jazz*," *Narrative* 11.2 (May 2003): 199–212; Mahboobeh Khaleghi, "Narration and Intertextuality in Toni Morrison's *Jazz*," *The Criterion: An International Journal in English* 2.1 (April 2011): 1–10.

13 As Morrison remarks in an interview: "In the first edition [of *Jazz*] the plot was on the cover, so that a person in a bookstore could read the cover and know right away what the book was about, and could, if they wished, dismiss it and buy another book. This seemed a suitable technique for *Jazz* because I thought of the plot in that novel – the threesome – as the melody of the piece, and it is fine to follow a melody – to feel the satisfaction of recognizing a melody whenever the narrator returns to it. That was the real art of the enterprise for me: bumping up against that melody time and again, seeing it from another point of view, seeing it afresh each time, playing it back and forth. . . . I wanted the story to be the vehicle which moved us from page one to the end, but I wanted the delight to be found in moving away from the story and coming back to it, looking around it, and through it, as though it were a prism, constantly turning.

   This playful aspect of *Jazz* may well cause a great deal of dissatisfaction in readers who just want the melody, who want to know what happened, who did it and why. But the jazz-like structure wasn't a secondary thing for me – it was the raison d'etre of the book. The process of trial and error by which the narrator revealed the plot was as important and exciting to me as telling the story." Toni Morrison, "The Art of Fiction CXXXIV," *The Paris Review* 128 (Fall 1993): 110–112.

14 Morrison, "The Art of Fiction," p. 116.

15 The nine founding families call themselves "8-Rock" because they are dark-skinned. "A deep deep level in the coal mines. Blue-black people, tall and graceful, whose clear, wide eyes gave no sign of what they really felt about those who weren't 8-rock like them." Toni Morrison, *Paradise* (New York: Knopf, 1998), p. 193. Subsequent references will be to this edition.

16 Lucille P. Fultz, *Toni Morrison: Playing with Difference* (Urbana and Chicago: University of Illinois Press, 2003), p. 93.

17   *Paradise* was the second of Morrison's books to have been featured in the Book Club. The others were *Song of Solomon* in 1996, *The Bluest Eye* in 2000, and *Sula* in 2002.

18   For a detailed reading of the *Paradise* episode of Oprah's Book Club, see Michael Perry, "Resisting Paradise: Toni Morrison, Oprah Winfrey, and the Middlebrow Audience," in *The Oprah Affect: Critical Essays on Oprah's Book Club*, ed. Cecilia Konchar Farr and Jaime Harker (Albany: State University of New York Press, 2008), pp. 119–139, and Timothy Aubry, "Beware the Furrow of the Middlebrow: Searching for *Paradise* on *The Oprah Winfrey Show*," in *The Oprah Affect*, pp. 163–187.

19   In "Recitatif," Morrison tells the stories of Twyla and Roberta. We first meet them when they are 8 years of age and staying at an orphanage during the 1950s. The story is organized around several chance re-encounters between the two that occur during the next couple of decades. Although we learn early in the story that the girls are of different races, we never learn which is black and which is white. The story challenges readers both to acknowledge the ways in which we make meaning both in literature and in life by assigning racial codes and to recognizing the de-stabilizing effect that is produced when those codes are removed. Second, her characterizations of Roberta and Twyla reveal the deep connections between constructions of class and race; readers' generalizations about race may actually apply as easily to socioeconomic status, and vice versa. Toni Morrison, "Recitatif," in *Confirmation: An Anthology of African American Women*, ed. Imamu Amiri Baraka and Amina Baraka (New York: William Morrow, 1983), pp. 243–261.

20   Aubry, p. 165.

21   Patricia is the daughter of Roger Best – an 8-Rock descendant – and his late wife Delia, a woman the men of Ruby despised because "she was a wife with no last name, a wife without people, a wife of sunlight skin, a wife of racial tampering" (p. 197). Delia died in childbirth because the town's midwives lacked the skills to handle the complications, and men of the town would not ask a white person for help, and the women could not drive.

22   Fultz, p. 98.

CHAPTER 5

Books for Young Readers, *Love* and *A Mercy*

From her earliest to her most recent novels, Toni Morrison displays a remarkable insightfulness into the minds of children, especially the minds of young African American girls. Whether she writes about children in the colonial period or the Jim Crow era, she captures their wisdom and vulnerability, innocence and sexuality, naivete and sophistication. The lives of children in her novels provide a window into the pathologies of the adult world. They are the canaries in the mine of American culture; their psychological and spiritual health is an index of the health of the communities within which they live. When we consider the lives of Pecola, Frieda, and Claudia of *The Bluest Eye*, Nel and Sula, Roberta and Twyla of "Recitatif," Beloved and Denver, Christine and Heed the Night in *Love*, and Florens in *A Mercy*, we can see how adult experiences of trauma are visited upon the children.

Given the central role children occupy in Morrison's fiction, it is not surprising that she would turn her hand to writing for young readers. From 1999 to 2004, Morrison collaborated with her son Slade Morrison and two artists (Giselle Potter on the first book and Pascale LeMaitre on the other four) on five books for young readers.[1] In 2004, she published *Remember: The Journey to School Integration*, a blend of archival photographs, historical background, and fictional narrative that captures the inner lives of African American students in the transition from segregated to integrated schools.

Toni Morrison: Writing the Moral Imagination, First Edition. Valerie Smith.
© 2012 Valerie Smith. Published 2014 by John Wiley & Sons, Ltd.

Her first five books for young readers have generally received mixed reviews. By giving voice to the child's point of view, criticizing the adult perspective, and refusing tidy moral endings, the books flout the conventions of children's literature. As a result, some publishers were reluctant to publish the books, some parents have questioned their appropriateness for children, and some reviewers have remarked that the books seem more directed toward adults than children.[2] Yet she and Slade Morrison, in collaboration with their illustrators, are after something other than merely meeting genre assumptions. The project of her books for young readers is consistent with that of her novels. In both cases, she encourages an active, participatory mode of reading and makes space for acts of resistance to cultural norms.

The Big Box (1999) and *The Book of Mean People* (2002) are picture books. *The Big Box* features three children – Patty, Mickey, and Liza Sue – who do the sorts of things average, middle-class American children do. Patty refuses to play with dolls, Mickey yells in the hallways and plays handball in front of the sign forbidding the game, and Liza Sue has too much fun outdoors and lets the chickens keep their eggs instead of collecting them. Their playfulness, imagination, and disregard for the rules adults impose upon them land them in the brown box – a lavishly appointed room with three locks which to them feels like a prison – because they cannot "handle their freedom."[3] In her interview with Rob Capriccioso, Morrison suggests that parents often find the book threatening because it subtly critiques the impulse to indulge children with material things while denying them attention or opportunities to explore the world on their own.

The various settings in the book display the differences between the children's fantasy world and the box in which they find themselves. The natural world where "seagulls scream," "rabbits hop," and "beavers chew trees when they need 'em" (p. 6) contrasts with the room where the children live:

> Oh, it's pretty inside and the windows are wide
> With shutters to keep out the day.
> They have swings and slides and custom-made beds
> And the doors open only one way. (p. 2)

In one flashback scene, the children's fun is shown to make the adults nervous; in another, the adults confront them about their behavior.

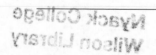

The children express some embarrassment for failing to conform to the wishes of the adults. But they also mention what they do right and point out their efforts to be obedient. In the poignant ending, they assert their right to independence:

> I don't mean to be rude: I want to be nice.
> But I'd like to hang on to my freedom.
>
> I know you are smart and I know that you think
> You are doing what is best for me.
> But if freedom is handled just your way
> Then it's not my freedom or free. (p. 34)

The Book of Mean People introduces the reader to the "mean" people in the life of a little bunny who is the main character and narrator: his parents, sibling, friends, and grandparents, among others. While the book is certainly a gentle critique of those who intimidate, tease, cajole, yell, gossip, and criticize, it is also the story of a bunny/child learning to navigate the paradoxes and ambiguities of adult speech and actions. (Morrison has remarked that the sorts of questions the bunny asks are inspired by the ones Slade Morrison asked when he was a child.) In most of the illustrations, the bunny carries with him a copy of a book called *The Book of Mean People.* The illustrations suggest that that book will help him make sense of the contradictory messages adults transmit, such as: "How can I sit down and sit up at the same time?" (p. 18). "How can I waste time if I use it?" (p. 34). As an assertion of his independence, in the final pages the bunny remarks that although he is frightened of frowning people when they smile, "I will smile anyway!" (p. 43).[4] In the final image he has removed his clothing and hops off into the woods, still holding his copy of *The Book of Mean People,* his puppy scampering at his heels.

The next three books comprise the *Who's Got Game?* series: *The Ant or the Grasshopper?* (2003), *The Lion or the Mouse?* (2003), and *Poppy or the Snake?* (2004). In these books, the Morrisons update Aesop's fables in a comic format using humor, contemporary vernacular, and syntax in tales with open-ended morals. The first re-tells a fable attributed to Aesop in which the grasshopper spends the warm months making music while the ant stores up food for the winter. When winter comes, the grasshopper finds himself starving and appeals to the ant for help, only to be chided for his improvidence. The fable is typically understood to teach the value of hard work and frugality. In the Morrisons' version, however, the grasshopper (Foxy G) and the ant (Kid A) begin the summer spending time together in a city park: swimming and playing basketball and air guitar. But as the summer progresses, Kid A realizes that he needs to prepare for the winter months, so he begins storing food and preparing his home. Foxy G wants to play music instead; as Kid A stocks and secures his home for himself and his family, he cannot help but be moved by Foxy G's sound. When the weather turns bitter cold, Foxy G realizes that his wings are freezing and crumbling and he can no longer make music. He goes to Kid A's home to ask for help, but his "friend" only mocks him for failing to prepare for winter.

At this point, the Morrisons' version departs from Aesop's. In an eloquent plea for the power of art and the role of the artist in society, Foxy G says:

> I quenched your thirst and fed your soul,
> You can't spare me a doughnut hole?. . . .
> I'm an artist, that's what I do!
> You loved my music so respect me too! . . .
> How can you say I never worked a day? Art is work
> It just looks like play.[5]

For a couple of pages the ant and the grasshopper debate the merits of their choices. After the ant turns the grasshopper away, Foxy G trudges away in the snow and reflects on his situation:

> His day is darkest when I leave
> With all my music up my sleeve.
> Name, fame, blame, shame –
> The question is: who's got game? (p. 20)

In the final image, Kid A gazes longingly out the window of his cozy family home as the figure of his former friend disappears into the snowy night. Rather than leaving readers with a tidy ending about the virtues of hard work and economy, the books asks whether either way alone is best; the ideal path might be a collaboration or partnership between the two.

At the start of the original version of the fable called "The Lion and the Mouse," a mouse runs up and down the body of a sleeping lion. When the lion awakens, he opens his jaws to swallow the mouse; the mouse begs for his life, warning the lion that one day he might need his help. The lion is so amused by the idea that the tiny mouse might actually be able to help him that he frees him. Some time afterward, the lion is caught in a trap. The mouse passes by and seeing the lion's predicament, he gnaws away at the ropes that ensnare him. The moral of the story: "Little friends may prove big friends."[6]

As in *The Ant or the Grasshopper?,* in *The Lion or the Mouse?* the Morrisons flesh out characters and give them strong personalities. At the start of the book, the lion is a fierce, boastful figure who brags in rhymes about his power and invincibility:

> I am the strongest night and day,
> I can whip anyone who gets in my way.
> Tigers, hyenas, elephants too,
> Everybody does what I say do.[7]

Everything changes when he gets a thorn in his paw that he cannot remove. All of a sudden, his threatening roar becomes a barely audible whisper as he pleads for help. All the larger animals pass him by; only the mouse, the smallest of them all, stops to offer him assistance. Because he is so small he is able to extract the thorn with his teeth. Filled with gratitude, the lion promises that they will be friends forever and that he will never eat the mouse.

The next day the mouse awakens filled with pride at his accomplishment and begins to carry himself as if he were now the lion. He now boasts of his prowess, but the other animals only laugh at him. Day after day he visits the lion to complain that no one takes him seriously; the lion creates a mane for him out of his own mane, cuts a piece of velvet from his robe to give the mouse a more imposing tongue, and makes a pair of boots for him that look like paws. But each embellishment only further provokes the other animals' derision. Finally, the lion gives the mouse his throne, his robe, and his crown in hopes that they will satisfy him, and the lion goes out to live in the jungle. In the end, while the mouse squeaks all day along about his power, the lion sings "a wiser song":

The biggest bully in the land
Does what he likes, takes what he can
. . . believes the sizes of boots and paws
are all you need to make the laws.
But strong or weak, big or small, a giant or an elf . . .
Is he who wants to be a bully just scared to be himself? (pp. 26–27)

To date, the last in the *Who's Got Game?* series is *Poppy or the Snake?* This one retells the story of the farmer and the frozen viper in which a farmer finds a snake in the snow. In the original version, the farmer places the snake inside his coat to warm it, and the snake comes back to life. Once the snake is revived, he bites the farmer. In this fable, the moral is that kindness is wasted on the evil.[8] The Morrisons' version likewise involves an encounter between a farmer and a snake, but in this case that story is embedded within a story involving a young African American boy named Nate and his grandfather, Poppy. The book opens with a conversation between Nate and Poppy from which we learn that Nate visits Poppy in his small house in the country every summer. Usually he is eager to return home and begin the new school year, but this summer he is reluctant because he has been failing to get good grades. Poppy tells him the story of his "remembering boots" to inspire him.[9]

As the story goes, one evening Poppy returned to his pickup truck after a day spent fishing only to discover that he had parked his truck on top of a poisonous snake. The snake begs Poppy to move the truck and free him; once the snake has been freed, he persuades Poppy to take him to his house and feed him. Before long, Poppy agrees to let the snake stay at his house to recuperate, ostensibly believing that he can trust the snake not to bite him because he has saved his life. But one morning he awakens and discovers that he has been bitten. When he asks the snake why he had broken his promise, the snake says simply: "Hey, Man, I'm a snake. You knew that" (p. 26). The book then returns to the frame narrative, in which Nate asks Poppy how he managed to survive the bite. As it turns out, Poppy had taken snake serum as a precaution. The moral he wants his grandson to understand as he begins the next school year is the value of preparedness. Poppy then puts his feet, shod in the remembering boots, on the table, and Nate observes that "they were beautiful and made of the softest, shiniest snakeskin" (p. 28).

Morrison's *Remember: The Journey to School Integration* is a strikingly different project from her other books for young readers. This book is filled with arresting, mostly full-page archival photographs of black and white children and adults involved in one way or other in the transition from Jim Crow segregation to school integration. *Remember: The Journey to School Integration*, is her first historical book for young readers. Composed of black-and-white photographs taken primarily from the 1940s until the 1970s and written text in which Morrison imagines "the thoughts and feelings of some of the people in the photographs,"[10] *Remember* takes readers inside the experience of Jim Crow schooling and the early days of integration.

The three-page introductory section, entitled "The Narrow Path, the Open Gate, the Wide Road," contains text surrounded by photographic images drawn from the full-size photographs found throughout the rest of the book. On the first page, pictures of black children – one in profile who appears to be listening, another who looks out from behind a fence, and a third who reads aloud from a book – are placed along the left-side of the page. Three images of white people are arrayed along the right side – a young girl in profile, a benign-looking white woman in profile, and a young white boy facing the camera.[11] From the opening sentences of this first section, it seems that the book intends to connect young readers with the history of school desegregation, to ensure that they understand the relevance of the *Brown* decision for their own lives, and that they understand that the past is part of who they are:

> This book is about you. Even though the main event in the story took place many years ago, what happened before it and after it is now part of all our lives. Because remembering is the mind's first step toward understanding, this book is designed to take you on a journey through a time in American life when there was as much hate as there was love; was much anger as there was hope; as many heroes as cowards. A time when people were overwhelmed with emotion and children discovered new kinds of friendships and a new kind of fear. As with any journey, there is often a narrow path to walk before you can see the wide road ahead. And sometimes there is a closed gate between the path and the road. (p. iii)

With this opening paragraph, the reader is prompted to understand that the present is linked seamlessly to the past and that what happened years ago continues to exert a profound impact on today's circumstances. The duty of the current generation is thus to remember the events of the past. Strikingly, Morrison does not invite her readers to "learn" or to "understand." She does not encourage them to acquire information. Rather, she prompts them to remember, as if they are already in possession of this knowledge. This use of the idea of memory is collective as well as intimate. Here, she affirms that memory is not merely the capacity to recall one's own experiences. Rather, she asserts that readers must take responsibility for learning about the past and make it part of their own storehouse of memories.

This introductory section begins on a positive note. The opening paragraph quoted above alludes to a time when hate was as prevalent as love, anger as hope, heroes as cowards. Were those terms reversed, with positive term going first in each pair, one might argue that from her perspective, the present fares poorly in comparison with the past. Given that the positive term follows the negative in each instance, however, she seems to suggest that conditions have improved since *Brown.*

The introduction highlights some of the themes that recur in other literature about the *Brown* decision. Although Morrison never uses this language explicitly, she intimates that school desegregation was the first battle of the modern Civil Rights Movement and that it was waged by ordinary parents and children. Further, she notes the shame associated with segregated schooling: however humiliating the other practices might have been, "nothing was more painful than being refused a decent education" (p. iii). On the second page, Morrison briefly summarizes the *Brown* decision and the movement that follows. As the account mentions acts of violence and intimidation, the photographs become more menacing. On this page, there are only two photographs of black students. In the lower left corner of the page is the head of Elizabeth Eckford of the Little Rock Nine, cropped from the famous photograph of her walking alone outside of Central High School, a crowd of angry whites at her back. In the upper right is a photograph of a young black boy looking rather apprehensive. The other photographs are of white people – a young white boy in a Klan robe, a white male teen looking vaguely menacing, an angry white woman screaming epithets, and a white boy looking somewhat amused.

Morrison begins the final page of the introduction with the following sentences: "Why offer memories you do not have? Remembering can be painful, even frightening. But it can also swell your heart and open your mind" (p. v). By referring to the Movement as part of their memories, rather than part of their history, she writes readers into more intimate relationship with the events, as if it is part of their own lives. And indeed, since we are the beneficiaries of these events, they do stand in intimate relation to us. The section concludes with an intermingling of her own memories of the period and of the decision and of ours. The images here include a young black girl dressed for school, a smiling black girl and a smiling black woman, a rather severe looking white woman and a pensive photograph of Dr. Martin Luther King, Jr. in profile. On this page she writes:

> Whenever I see sheets drying on the line or smell gumbo simmering on the stove, a flood of memories comes back to me. In 1953 when I traveled in the rural South with a group of students, we received the generosity of strangers – African Americans who took us in when there were no places for nonwhites to eat or sleep. . . . The joy I felt in 1954, when the Supreme Court decided the *Brown v. Board of Education* case, was connected to those generous strangers, and even now wind-dried sheets can summon up my memory of what that decision did and what it meant for all our futures. This book is a celebration of the power and justice of that decision.

> So remember. Because you are a part of it. The path was not entered, the gate was not opened, the road was not taken only for those brave enough to walk it. It was for you as well. In every way, this is your story. (p. v)

The text thus invites the reader into an empathic relation with the events it describes. Readers are encouraged to encounter the experience as if it is their own, to imagine themselves into the situations presented photographically, and then to commit themselves to a persistent act of recall.

Remember is divided into three sections, "The Narrow Path," "The Open Gate," and "The Wide Road." Most of the photographs in the first section are of black children under the Jim Crow system; the accompanying text imagines what they might be thinking and thus helps a young reader imagine herself under those conditions. The first image in this section, for example, shows a class of young black children in Washington, DC in 1942. One young girl in the front row, wearing a dress and ankle socks and with a ribbon in her hair, stands reading aloud from a book. The accompanying text reads: "The law says I can't go to school with white children. Are they afraid of my socks, my braids? I am seven years old. Why are they afraid of me?" (p. 8).

The second section, "The Open Gate," focuses on the decision and its aftermath, including pictures of the front page of the *New York Times* on May 18, 1954 as well as of the entire Warren Court. The early photographs display tranquil images of integrated groups of students. These images soon give way to a series of images in which white resistance to the decision is in evidence.

In the final section, "The Wide Road," the book opens up to images of Jim Crow culture and the Civil Rights Movement: segregated facilities, people marching with placards, sitting at lunch counters, Rosa Parks on a desegregated bus, Dr. King at the March on Washington. As this section ends, images of black and white children happily in classes together re-emerge. In the antepenultimate image, a young black boy draws a picture of what he calls "Magic Man" on the blackboard. The caption reads: "I am drawing a Magic Man. He can make anything happen. Anything at all. Just wait and see" (p. 69). The next image features a black girl and a white girl holding hands through the school bus window with a caption that reads: "Anything can happen. Anything at all. See?" (p. 71). The book concludes with the dedicating page to the four girls who were killed in the Sixteenth Street Baptist Church in Birmingham, AL in 1963. Their photographs are accompanied by a sentence that identifies them and a caption that reads: "Things are better now./Much, much better./But remember why and please/remember us. *Their lives short, their deaths quick. Neither were in vain* (p. 72).

Love

The central figure in the Foreword to *Love,* Morrison's eighth novel, is an enigmatic friend from her childhood. When they were young, Morrison found this girl pretty but remote, wise beyond her years, melancholy, and uninterested in boys. Later on, Morrison and her friends learn that this girl's odd behavior was likely the result of the fact that she had been betrayed by her father, who had habitually molested her. As Morrison writes, in retrospect, this realization marked a turning point in their development:

> Before we even knew who we were, someone we trusted our lives to could, might, would make use of our littleness, our ignorance, our need, and sully us to the bone, disturbing the balance of our lives as theirs had clearly been disturbed.[12]

Elsewhere in the Foreword, Morrison expands the scope of her meditation on the nature of betrayal to consider its place in the political arena, specifically during the era of the long Civil Rights revolution. Typically, the narrative of the Civil Rights era is understood as a triumph over white supremacy, a political ideology enacted through a system of laws and cultural practices designed to relegate non-whites to a second-class status, thus withholding from them their rights as citizens. But that narrative also depends upon the illusion, if not the fact, of intraracial loyalty and consensus. It presupposes a shared sense of unity among African Americans in the face of white oppression. In *Love*, however, Morrison provides a counter narrative, turning her readers' attention to the network of allegiances and deceptions, trust and duplicity that shaped the relationships among black people – especially between black men and women – throughout the years of the freedom struggle. From the perspective of a cluster of economically, sexually, and psychically vulnerable women, the novel explores the connection between love and betrayal at the levels of cultural, political, and personal experience.

The plot of *Love* revolves around a character named Bill Cosey, the wealthy African American owner of a hotel and night club in a seaside town called Up Beach that catered to black guests during the era of segregation. A savvy, entrepreneurial figure, Cosey is generous to his poor and working-class African American neighbors while keeping them at a social distance; he is solicitous of the wealthy whites who live in his community. The action of the novel flows from his 1942 marriage to Heed the Night Johnson, his granddaughter Christine's best friend, when Heed is only 11. This marriage destroys the girls' relationship and triggers a rivalry between the two of them that lasts until the moments before Heed's death as an elderly woman at the end of the novel. Not only do they compete for Cosey's love, but they also fight over the right to his home located at One Monarch Street in the town of Silk. His intended beneficiary is unclear because Cosey's only known will leaves the property to "my sweet Cosey child" (p. 4), an appellation to which both women lay claim.

Rumor has it that either Christine or Heed poisoned Cosey, but by the end of the novel we learn that the real murderer is L, the cook at Cosey's restaurant whose posthumous, italicized narration haunts the text. L reveals that she poisoned Cosey in order to prevent him from executing his legitimate will, in which he bequeathed his house to his long-time lover, the prostitute Celestial. At Cosey's death in 1971, L destroys his will and replaces it with a counterfeit written on the back of a 1958 menu from the restaurant at Cosey's resort.

The structure of *Love* would seem to suggest that the novel is about Cosey and his charismatic power. Each of the nine sections into which the book is divided is named for a role Cosey occupies in the minds of others – Portrait, Friend, Stanger, Benefactor, Lover, Husband, Guardian, Father, and Phantom. Moreover, to varying degrees, the women characters – Heed, Christine, Junior Viviane, Celestial, May, Vida, and L – are enthralled by the literal and symbolic force of his personality. As the novel unfolds, it becomes increasingly clear that *Love* is more concerned with the destructive impact of patriarchal power upon the women and their relationships with each other, than it is with Cosey himself. The figure of L and the secret that is only revealed in the final pages re-focus the reader's attention on the buried story, the powerful girlhood friendship between Heed and Christine. By the end of the novel, we understand that by betraying that relationship, Cosey has relegated both women to a lifetime of trauma and despair.

The present action of *Love* takes place in 1995 and comprises the period beginning with Junior Viviane's arrival in Silk (the town near which Cosey's Hotel and Resort is located) and ending with Heed's reconciliation with Christine as she lies dying in Christine's arms. Although much of the novel is devoted to events in the narrative present, more of it looks back on the period from the 1920s to the 1970s, the backstory to the characters' current circumstances. As a result, for much of the novel, the reader is carried forward in time with only a partial understanding of why characters behave and events transpire as they do. As we move forward in time, we learn more about the past.

We have seen this resistance to the forward movement of chronology in other Morrison novels, most notably in *Jazz* and *Paradise.* As Jean Wyatt has argued, however, the "temporal disorder" of *Love* is inextricably tied to the traumatic events on which the novel centers and that are only revealed late in the book. The "temporal disorder" is an aesthetic expression of the wound Christine and Heed sustained when Christine saw Cosey masturbating in her bedroom, and when Cosey molested and then married Heed when he was 52 and she was only 11. By awakening them to their sexuality prematurely, he wreaks havoc on the girls' psychosexual development, disrupting each girl's relationship to her own body and subjectivity as well as her orderly passage into adult womanhood. Furthermore, his actions destroy Heed's and Christine's rich childhood friendship, thereby ruining their capacity to forge and sustain relationships with others for the rest of their lives.[13]

Love opens with the first of five italicized sections told from L's point of view. As early as the first sentence, L describes her voice as a "hum," the only discursive register available to her at the end of the twentieth century now that silence, discretion, and indirection have lost the power they once possessed. Her section functions as an overture to the novel, introducing themes, situations, motifs, and characters that gain significance as the novel unfolds. Here she alludes to psychic wounds that cannot heal; a woman who buries a purchase deed in her father-in-law's beachfront property (May); foxglove (the poison she used to murder Cosey); and fish odor and integration (Cosey's and May's explanations for what ruined the resort's business).

More importantly, L suggests how her sections ought to be read in relation to those narrated from the other characters' perspectives. While the titled chapters in roman font are comparatively straightforward and accessible, they exemplify L's view of late twentieth-century discourse where *"all is known and nothing understood"* (p. 4). In those sections reside accessible, convenient explanations for complex emotions. In those sections, characters attribute unfathomable suffering to "outside evil," as exemplified by the Police-heads, "dirty things with big hats who shoot up out of the ocean to harm loose women and eat disobedient children" (p. 5). In contrast, L's sections are allusive and indirect; harder to comprehend, they are the places where difficult, hidden truths may be found. L compares her voice, her hum, to the soundtrack of a film, a sound that is present even when unnoticed, an accompaniment to the plot that directs our responses:

> *I'm background – the movie music that comes along when the sweethearts see each other for the first time, or when the husband is walking the beachfront alone wondering if anybody saw him doing the bad thing he couldn't help. My humming encourages people; frames their thoughts like when Mildred Pierce decides she has to go to jail for her daughter. I suspect, soft as it is, my music has that kind of influence too. The way "Mood Indigo" drifting across the waves can change the way you swim. It doesn't make you dive in, but it can set your stroke, or trick you into believing you are both smart and lucky. So why not swim farther and a little farther still? What's the deep to you? It's way down below, and has nothing to do with blood made bold by coronets and piano keys, does it?* (p. 4)

At first glance, L seems to have a clearer vision of the history of the community and of the other characters. However, like them she longs for the years before the social and cultural changes ushered in by the Civil Rights era. In her view, people in the 1990s – especially African Americans – have lost many of the qualities that fortified their ancestors and bound them together into strong communities. Fearful of the cycles of nature and lacking resourcefulness, they have become overly dependent upon the state for protection. Tied to jobs and sources of entertainment miles away from home, they spend more time in their cars than they do in their neighborhoods. She yearns for a time when a black-owned resort could attract top entertainers and black elites would flock to such a place to enjoy each other's company. The poorly built homes thrown up in the name of urban renewal pale in comparison to the quality of the construction of her own shack.

It should not surprise us that this novel, set in 1995, features a host of characters who look back longingly to the Jim Crow era. In the late twentieth and early twenty-first centuries, with an increase in black-on-black crime, a persistent gap in black and white wealth and in black and white educational achievements, and the displacement of African American communities due to the gentrification of urban areas across the nation, it has become increasingly common for blacks to express some nostalgia for the days of segregation, when black communities were supposedly more unified and cohesive. Cosey's daughter-in-law May, who died well before the narrative present begins, articulates the most extreme version of this longing. The emotionally fragile, genteel daughter of an itinerant preacher, she anchors herself to Cosey's wealth and family history of independence and entrepreneurship, and she will do anything to keep her connection to the financial security he represents. She sees threats to her hard-won material prosperity everywhere. Terrified not only of black nationalists but also of the nonviolent activists associated with the mainstream Civil Rights struggle, she blames the Civil Rights Movement for destroying the family business and the family itself.

Sandler and Vida Gibbons, Cosey's former employees, likewise long for earlier times. Although Vida makes more money as a hospital aide, she misses the contentment of working as a receptionist at Cosey's Hotel; like so many of the women who had lived and worked in Up Beach, she adored him and saw in him the pinnacle of African American achievement. As a young man, Sandler understood that Cosey and the elites to whom he catered maintained a strict social separation from working people like himself. But like the other local people, he admired Cosey and his guests vicariously nevertheless; their luxury offered an alternative to the cruel exclusions of racial segregation. For him as for L, dissatisfaction with contemporary architecture symbolizes his longing for the past. His drafty, "government-improved and approved housing" (p. 39) is shabbily built when compared to the humble shack he and Vida left behind when they moved to town. And just as L misses the nuances of language, Sandler misses the subtleties of light. His new neighborhood is so completely saturated with streetlamps that he can no longer experience the sounds and smells of a wood-burning fire and rich play of moonlight:

> As he did almost every day, as now, on a very cold night, longing for the crackle of fire in a stingy potbelly stove, the smell of clean driftwood burning. He couldn't forget the picture the moon turned those Up Beach cabins into . . . The planners believed that dark people would do fewer dark things if there were twice as many streetlamps as anywhere else. Only in fine neighborhoods and the country were people entrusted to shadow. So even when the moon was full and blazing, for Sandler it was like a bounty hunter's far-off torch, not the blanket of beaten gold it once spread over him and the ramshackle house of his childhood, exposing the trick of the world, which is to make us think it is ours. (p. 39)

This nostalgia is bound up with the hero worship that gives Cosey so much power in his community. Cosey's self-absorption and abusiveness are extreme expressions of his patriarchal power. Portrait, Friend, Stranger, Benefactor, Lover, Husband, Guardian, Father, and Phantom – he occupies all of these categories at once; the acts of betrayal around which the novel revolves stem from circumstances that result from the disintegration of the boundaries that separate these roles.

Cosey's power is so far-reaching that it consumes even Junior Viviane, a young woman who never even met him while he was alive. Junior is scarred both literally and figuratively by her childhood in the Settlement, a place the narrator describes as "a planet away from the Monarch Street" (p. 53). The Settlement is inhabited by poor, uneducated, violent people who value nothing more than loyalty. For them, "the only crime was departure" (p. 55). Junior's name came from an offhand comment from her father who disappeared shortly after her birth. So desperate is she for the love of this man – about whom she knows only that he was in the US Army – that her search for him takes over her imaginary life. Her wild uncles drive over her foot when they fear that she is making friendships outside the Settlement; once she recovers from her injury, she runs away from home. She might have gone undetected indefinitely had she not stolen a G. I. Joe doll and refused to return it, a doll she treasures because it becomes a symbol of her father. After years spent in "the Correctional" – where her sentence is extended after she almost kills the administrator who sexually assaults her – Junior comes to Silk seeking work in the Cosey home in response to a Help Wanted advertisement. While she initiates an intensely sexual relationship with Romen, Sandler and Vida's grandson, more importantly, she also comes under Cosey's spell.

After seeing his portrait on the wall above Heed's bed, she recognizes Cosey in the dream she had the first night she spent in the house. He appears as a reassuring presence in her recurring phallic nightmare in which upright snakes try to lure her down from a tree. The next day she discovers his room – an office where his clothing and personal effects are kept – across the hall from hers. In the room of "her Good Man" (as she calls him), she loses herself in the sensual experience of his possessions, stroking his clothing, smelling his shoes, and "[rubbing] her cheek on the sleeve of his seersucker jacket" (p. 119). When she finds his underwear, she removes her clothing, puts on a pair of his shorts, and pleasures herself on his sofa. "Her Good Man" soon becomes a specter that haunts her waking life as well. Through her sensual and psychological engagement with him, he is as present to her as Romen is. She feels his "unmistakable" happiness in her company and believes she sees the cuff of his shirtsleeve closing the door shortly before she spots Romen for the first time. She senses him watching and encouraging her, whispering: " 'Nice hair,' 'Take it,' 'Good girl,' 'Sweet tits,' 'Why not?' " (p. 116). Her fixation on Cosey recalls the convergence of the paternal and the erotic in his relationship with Heed and Christine. For Junior as well for them, he becomes Lover and Father, Phantom and Guardian, Stranger and Friend.

The full impact of Cosey's power and narcissism becomes evident in the lives of Heed and Christine. Heed is a Johnson, a member of an impoverished, illiterate, uncouth family all-too-willing to sell their daughter to Cosey for $200 and a pocketbook. May tried to keep the girls apart, fearful that the association would contaminate her daughter. But despite their socioeconomic differences, each of these lonely girls sees something of herself in the other, and they are bound together through this identification, a profound love and a shared private language. They speak idagay to each other when they want to share secrets.[14] And after the beautiful prostitute Celestial winks at the two 10-year-old girls while ignoring the man who calls her name, Heed and Christine adopt the phrase "Hey, Celestial" in order to "acknowledge a particularly bold, smart, risky thing" (p. 188).

"Hey, Celestial" not only recalls the thrill of being recognized by this woman who has earned the disapprobation of the respectable women in the community, but it also marks the girls' safe and playful initiation, through verbal indirection, into the world of sexuality. When the man calls her name, they detect a touch of humor, private knowing, and envy. Celestial disregards him, turning her beautiful face marred only by a fine scar that runs from cheek to ear, and winks at them; the delicate balance of joy, fear, and the unknown thrills them. In their preadolescent world of play, they use this private code phrase at will to recall the excitement of the moment.

Their relationship and indeed, their lives, begin to disintegrate on the summer day in 1940 about which they are unable to speak. The day starts out as any other; the girls play on the beach in the abandoned rowboat they have named the Celestial Palace. Wearing Christine's swimsuits and matching hairstyles, playing and eating their picnic lunch, Heed and Christine are as close as twins. But everything changes when Heed runs back into the hotel to retrieve their set of jacks. As she wiggles her hips in time to the music she hears coming from the hotel bar, she runs into Mr. Cosey, who pinches the place where her nipple will soon emerge. Shocked by the feeling his touch arouses, she races back outside to tell Christine, only to find her friend hiding behind the hotel with vomit on her bathing suit. Fearing that Christine has been made ill by seeing her grandfather's touch, she believes that the sensation she felt was wrong and that she is responsible because of her hip-wriggling. What she does not know is that Christine has just experienced a violation of her own.

On the verge of yelling up to her open bedroom window to urge Heed to hurry back, she sees her grandfather at the bedroom window, masturbating. She does not understand what she sees, but this displacement of her best friend by her grandfather, and the vision of his orgasm, spontaneously causes her to vomit. When she goes to bed that night, she feels that his presence has invaded her room and cannot be exorcised:

> His shadow had booked the room. She didn't have to glance at the window or see the curtains yield before a breeze to know that an old man's solitary pleasure lurked there. Like a guest with a long-held reservation arriving in your room at last, a guest you knew would stay. (p. 192)

Like Heed, Christine is worried more by the sense of shame and guilt than she is by the arousal she feels. Both girls are haunted by the fear that "the inside dirtiness" will "leak" (p. 192).

From here, the verbal and emotional connection between the two girls is irreparably broken, and they are permanently out of place in their own lives. Within a year, Cosey has decided to marry this prepubescent girl whose wedding gown is several sizes too big for her tiny frame. Still a child, she believes that her friend, his granddaughter, ought to be able to accompany her on her honeymoon. Too fearful and vulnerable to criticize Cosey for making this obscene choice, May and Christine lash out at Heed and ridicule her for her ignorance. Heed spends her life seeking acceptance, forced to fill a woman's role when she is only a child, and unable to accept her maturity as she advances in age.[15] Christine is sent away from home repeatedly, partly to protect her from exposure to the "old-man business" (p. 133) in her grandfather's bedroom, and partly to avert conflict with Heed. In response, she moves from one destructive relationship with a man to the next, seeking substitutes for her lost place in her grandfather's home and affection. Only as Heed lies dying in Christine's arms do the two comprehend their common sense of violation and realize that their quest for love and freedom was really a search to return to the oneness of their girlhood friendship. As they observe near the end of the novel, their relationship was no match for Cosey's patriarchal power:

> We could have been living our lives hand in hand instead of looking for Big Daddy everywhere.
> He was everywhere. And nowhere.
> We make him up?
> He made himself up.
> We must have helped. (p. 189)

A Mercy

Although *A Mercy* is set in a much earlier historical period than any of Morrison's other novels, it has much in common with several of her other works. Centering on a household of women characters, it reminds us of *Song of Solomon, Paradise, Jazz,* and *Love.* With its focus on the consequences of a slave mother's sacrifice, it invites comparison with *Beloved.* Like *Love,* it addresses the consequences of the protagonist's early experience of abandonment and loss. But while Cosey deliberately betrays Heed and Christine, Florens's mother gives her away as an act of love.

Set in the Atlantic colonies during the late seventeenth century, Morrison's ninth novel, *A Mercy* (2008), focuses on a group of people brought together into a common household through a series of commercial transactions. The characters are multiethnic and multiracial, and include an Anglo-Dutch farmer, his English wife, a Portuguese Catholic plantation owner, and a workforce of Native, black, white, and mixed-race slaves, indentured servants, and a freedman. In the early years of their life together, the principal characters coexist in a state of mutual dependency, working together with great efficiency in order to create a world out of the wilderness. But greed sustained by powerful racial, gender, and class hierarchies contaminates their universe; greed is symbolically responsible for Jacob Vaark's death and the tragic upheaval of the lives of the women who depend upon him. Like most of Morrison's novels, *A Mercy* is told from multiple narrative perspectives; the meanings of the narrative emerge out of the interconnections among the different points of view. In this instance, through the convergence of her characters' stories, Morrison interrogates the meaning of freedom and enslavement, wilderness and civilization. The narrative structure of *A Mercy* thus resists the ideologies and hierarchies that destroy the Vaarks' lives and threaten Florens's, Lina's, and Sorrow's security.

A Mercy centers on a group of literally or symbolically orphaned characters who live and work together on the estate of Jacob Vaark, an Anglo-Dutch trader and landowner. An orphan himself, Jacob came to the colonies after inheriting a parcel of 120 acres of land from his uncle. His household comprises various individuals he has bought or hired. Messalina, called Lina, his first purchase, is a young Native woman orphaned when the plague killed off most of her people. Seeing in her someone to help him run his farm, Vaark buys Lina from the Presbyterians who had taken her in and tried to "civilize" her. Next, he essentially buys his wife, Rebekka, from her parents in England. In search of "an unchurched woman of childbearing age, obedient but not groveling, literate but not proud, independent but nurturing" (p. 20) to manage his household, he agrees to reimburse her parents for her personal effects. Third, he accepts Sorrow, a young girl of indeterminate racial origin, as partial payment from a sawyer who owes him money. A troubled young woman who converses with her alter ego, Twin, as a way of coping with her traumatic past, Sorrow had lived aboard a ship with a captain reputed to have been her father and survived a shipwreck before the sawyer rescues her and takes her into his home. After the sawyer's wife discovers that their sons have been sexually abusing Sorrow, she vows to get rid of her. Willard and Scully, two white men who work for Jacob, are likewise discards, both sold into servitude. The narrative present begins shortly before Jacob meets Florens, his final acquisition.

The novel is divided into 11 sections that alternate between Florens' first-person point of view and the perspectives of Jacob, Lina, Rebekka, Sorrow, Willard, and Scully, and a minha mae.[16] Narrated in the first person and in the present tense, Florens's sections refer to or describe the key incidents on which the novel focuses and tells the story of her journey to find her lover, the blacksmith. The other sections, narrated in third-person free indirect discourse and in the past tense, provide the characters' backstories, flesh out Florens's account, and reveal the interconnections that bind their lives into a community. This use of alternating perspectives illuminates the symbolic links among their personal histories and establishes the way of reading through analogy the novel requires.

As is the case in so many of Morrison's previous works, the opening section contains allusions to the plot and dominant motifs of the novel, references that acquire meaning in the course of reading and re-reading *A Mercy*. When we enter the world of the novel for the first time, however, we must give ourselves over to the disorientation of inhabiting a universe whose codes are unfamiliar. This experience of disorientation is especially significant when we realize that *A Mercy* is set in seventeenth-century Maryland, Virginia and New York and focuses primarily on a series of events that transpired in May 1690. As Morrison remarks in an interview, during that period, "what we now call America was fluid, ad hoc.[17] As a result, the novel is replete with scenes of characters confused, if not overwhelmed, by their environments and circumstances.[18] Their very survival depends upon their ability to make sense of and lay claim to the world within which they find themselves. Through their encounters and experiences, successes and defeats, Morrison dramatizes the challenges of entering a new world and seeking to make it one's own.

A Mercy begins where it ends. In the first section we meet Florens, the 16-year-old protagonist, where we leave her in the penultimate section of the novel: writing her life story on the floor, walls, and ceiling of a room in her late master's near-complete mansion, a home she has been forbidden to enter. She begins this project as a way of explaining her assault on Malaik, a foundling, to the blacksmith, the lover from whom she is estranged. As we learn later in the novel, in the process of inscribing the events that led her to dislocate the child's shoulder, Florens claims her autonomous identity as an adult woman, legally enslaved yet psychically free.

The opening section situates the narrative in its historical setting, identifies the principal characters, and introduces the dominant themes. It establishes Florens as a fervent young woman whose intensity has not been slaked by her status as a slave, and it presents the moment of separation from her mother from which she cannot recover. The need to compensate for this loss fuels both her intense passion for the blacksmith, her first lover, as well as her hostility toward Malaik.

Beyond these details of her personal story, the opening section also introduces several motifs that will prove to be significant to the novel as a whole: the central trope of new worlds, the critical issue of sexual victimization, and the ambiguous role of religion in the colonial period and in the system of slavery. The opening section also reveals the importance of literacy. Even though the law forbids slaves to learn (or be taught) to read and write, Florens is literate. Her mastery of these skills provides a means by which she creates and asserts the meaning of her existence. Her survival depends upon her ability to read a multiplicity of other codes as well. She knows how to interpret supernatural signs; her dreams of a minha mae and her little boy, or the shape of a dog's profile in the steam rising from a kettle, warn her of imminent danger. Given the rampant wilderness of this new world, she also learns to read the natural environment:

> I want to run across the trail through the beech and white pine but I am asking myself which way? Who will tell me? Who lives in the wilderness between this farm and you and will they help me or harm me? What about the boneless bears in the valley? Remember? How when they move their pelts sway as though there is nothing underneath? Their smell belying their beauty, their eyes knowing us from when we are beasts also. You telling me that is why it is fatal to look them in the eye. They will approach, run to us to love and play which we misread and give back fear and anger. (p. 5)

Finally, as a black enslaved woman, Florens must be able to read the social codes that govern her life. She quickly deduces that the Reverend Father, a Catholic priest, cannot protect her once they leave her home plantation. She immediately figures out that Lina will be her ally at the Vaark farm but that neither Rebekka not Sorrow has much use for her. And she knows that her own memory of her first encounter with Jacob underscores Lina's assessment of him:

> Lina says Sir has a clever way of getting without giving. I know it is true because I see it forever and ever. Me watching, my mother listening, her baby boy on her hip. Senhor is not paying the whole amount he owes to Sir. Sir saying he will take instead the woman and the girl, not the

baby boy and the debt is gone. A minha mae begs no. Her baby boy is still at her breast. Take the girl, she says, my daughter, she says. Me. Me. Sir agrees and changes the balance due. (p. 8)

This resonant passage confirms Florens's and Lina's ability to read the codes of domination under which they live. It introduces the metaphor of exchange that governs the lives of all who live at the Vaarks' farm. And it provides insight into Florens's use of the present tense. When she says she sees the scene of her mother giving her up "forever and ever," she admits that she can never move out of the traumatic moment that lives perpetually in her consciousness. The repetition of the word "Me" also bespeaks her incredulity that her mother would renounce her. This pivotal event becomes constitutive of who she is. Moreover, the use of the present tense is symbolic of the narrative mode of the novel. All the characters' pasts remain present. Despite their differences in race, ethnicity, or gender, their lives are deeply connected to each other.

On the one hand, by teaching Florens to read and write using the Nicene Creed and other sacred texts, the Reverend Father contributes to her autonomy and intellectual independence. But on the other hand, his teachings about the need to accommodate oneself to the conditions of one's captivity implicate him in the practice of domination. Indeed, throughout the novel, religious communities prove to be sites of cruelty that perpetuate dominance and racist ideology. Presbyterians impose their dubious "civilizing" project on Lina and almost succeed in convincing her of her own intrinsic sinfulness. The Anabaptists offer Rebekka no comfort upon the death of her children, but after the blacksmith saves her from smallpox, she affiliates herself with them. As Rebekka grows closer to that community, she ceases to recognize the humanity of the black and Native women who work for her.

Although the sections told from Florens's point of view might be said to tie the disparate perspectives together, the other narrators illuminate the details as well as the context of Florens's story. At the beginning of his chapter, Jacob is en route to Jublio, the lavish home of Senhor D'Ortega, a Catholic Portuguese trader and plantation owner in Maryland, to settle a debt. In contrast to the spartan, abstemious conditions on the Vaark farm, the D'Ortegas live far above their means, in a manner that Jacob both finds contemptible and envies. Lacking the money he needs to pay Jacob the money he owes him, D'Ortega offers him one of his slaves. But even though Jacob profits indirectly from the slave trade, he does not want to own an enslaved person. Furthermore, he does not want to accept a slave just to sell him or her, for "Flesh was not his commodity." To his mind, slaves are "too much trouble to transport, manage, auction; his solitary, unencumbered proficiency was what he liked about trade. Specie, bills of credit, quit claims, were portable. One satchel carried all he needed" (pp. 22–23).

Jacob's objection to the institution of slavery is thus not moral; it is essentially aesthetic. But he reluctantly agrees to accept a slave as payment when he realizes that D'Ortega is unlikely to offer him any other form of remuneration. Jacob chooses the clove-scented woman who cooks and serves their food. But D'Ortega refuses to let her go, saying that his wife cannot live without her cooking. (As Jacob suspects, and we learn later, D'Ortega will not let her go because both he and his wife sexually abuse her.) Jacob only agrees to take her daughter, Florens, after a minha mae drops to her knees and begs him to take Florens instead. This moment of apparent rejection becomes the defining trauma of Florens's life. Haunted by what she believes to be an act of abandonment, she is consumed by the desire for love and terrified by the prospect of losing it again. In her mother's eyes, however, Jacob's willingness to take her away is "a mercy;" she believes that going with Jacob will offer her daughter some modicum of protection from the sexual victimization to which she had been submitted in Barbados and at Jublio.

In addition to describing the circumstances under which he came to "acquire" Florens, Jacob also reveals something of the geographical, racial, and cultural landscape of the British Atlantic colonies. As he makes his way to Jublio, he acknowledges the fluidity of governance and land claims; he is never certain which nation or religion controls any specific area from 1 year or town to the next. As Morrison has remarked, in *A Mercy,* she was interested to "separate race from slavery to see what it was like, to be a slave but without being raced; where your status was being enslaved but there was no implication of racial inferiority."[19] Part of Jacob's fear of being in "Mary's land" comes from the fact that the nascent legal system established to secure the landed gentry and disrupt allegiances between blacks and Native people has created, rather than quelled, treacherous conditions.

Jacob also provides a perspective on the novel's symbolic geography. When we first meet him, he is enthralled by the natural landscape, the "sun fired fog turning the world into thick, hot gold" (p. 9), "forests untouched since Noah, shorelines beautiful enough to bring tears, wild food for the taking" (p. 12). After Jacob has come under the spell of the D'Ortega's opulent home, his avarice completely transforms his point of view. Not only does he now seek to justify his involvement with the slave trade, but the triangular slave trade provides metaphors for the home of which he dreams as well. It is a dream that depends upon the exploitation both of natural resources and of the labor of others. Where earlier he had been moved to tears over the vision of the landscape through which he travels, now he "fondles" the idea of imposing his will upon, dominating, and consuming the natural environment. His greed symbolizes the corruption at the heart of the American national mythology and is at least party responsible for his death.

The ensuing sections advance the narrative and underscore the dominant themes. As his great house is being completed, Jacob succumbs to smallpox. His final wish is to be taken into the house, and he draws his last breath as he crosses the threshold. Shortly afterward, Rebekka contracts the disease and sends Florens to find the blacksmith, the only person known to be able to provide a cure. Lina's section provides a rich sense of day-to-day life on the Vaarks' farm. She describes, for example, how hard Vaark worked before he found a wife, her own close relationship with Rebekka forged out of the experience of shared labor, and the impact of the new house upon all who work there. Distrustful of the new house, she believes that the spirit of waste and excess that produced it is responsible for the troubles they face: "Killing trees in that number, without asking their permission, of course his efforts would stir up malfortune" (p. 44). Although in many ways the Vaarks and those who work for them lead a privileged life, Lina is the first to realize how vulnerable the women are once Jacob dies. Since he and Rebekka have no male heirs – their three infant sons (as well as their daughter) have all died – if Rebekka dies, Lina, Florens, Sorrow, and Sorrow's baby will all be without a place.

Rebekka's section describes her life prior to, during, and after her transatlantic journey to the new world, further clarifying the similarities between her condition and that of the women who work for her. Daughter of a boatman all too ready to divest himself of the burden of an unmarried daughter, she was relegated to steerage along with seven other discarded women. Packed between pieces of luggage and next to the animal stalls, these "exiled, thrown-away" European women endure a modified Middle Passage (p. 82). Further, the ambiguous status of two of the seven – Elizabeth, "the daughter, or so she said, of an important Company agent" and Abigail, who was "quickly transferred to the captain's cabin" (p. 82) – helps to explain the uncertainty surrounding Sorrow's origins.

Although Rebekka's father is eager to ship her off to be married, her mother has her doubts about sending her to the colonies. Her religious convictions make her wary of marrying her daughter off to a man she considers a heathen, and she is fearful of life in the American wilderness. But Rebekka is "the stubborn one, the one with too many questions and a rebellious mouth" (p. 74). Recognizing her parents' lack of generosity toward family members and strangers alike, she cannot muster up much in the way of filial devotion. The Separatists' refusal to baptize her dying child only confirms her doubts about the depth and sincerity of their beliefs.

Rebekka not only questions the meaning, principles, and substance of religious belief and practice, but she also poses probing questions about the meaning and values associated with civilization. Her mother fears that the "savages and nonconformists" in the new world will slaughter her. But Rebekka understands that the raw brutality of public executions and the blood lust of the crowds who attend and re-live them in the retelling are part of daily life in London; nothing she will see in the colonies can equal the cruelty to which she has already been exposed. Instead of savagery and violence, she finds awe-inspiring beauty in the new world, and she revels in the pristine natural landscape.

Despite the loss of all her children, Rebekka is content with the fruits of her labor; she delights in Jacob's stories from his travels and the simple and functional gifts he brings her. But as his gifts become increasingly extravagant and his stories fewer and farther between, he asserts his patriarchal power over her and an irreparable rift opens between them.

Her earlier skepticism notwithstanding, Rebekka turns to religion after the blacksmith declares her healed. As Sorrow watches her pray, she sees a vision of Rebekka's isolation: "On her knees, her head bowed, she seemed completely alone in the world. Sorrow understood that servants, however many, would not make a difference. Somehow their care and devotion did not matter to her. So Mistress had no one – no one at all. Except the One she was whispering to: 'Thank you my Lord for the saving grace you have shown me' " (p. 130). Out of the vulnerability that comes with the death of her husband and the absence of an heir, Rebekka chooses to affiliate with the community of Anabaptists she had previously despised. Despite their shared history, she can no longer depend upon the women in her household. They are not in a position to provide protection for each other. And at the end of the day, Rebekka cannot overlook the racial differences that divide them. As she draws closer to the Anabaptists, she becomes diminished in spirit and increasingly cruel to the women who work for her; by the end of the novel, she is preparing to sell Sorrow and Florens. As Florens observes:

> Her heart is infidel. All smiles are gone. Each time she returns home from the meetinghouse her eyes are nowhere and have no inside. Like the eyes of the women who examine me behind the closet door, Mistress' eyes only look out and what she is seeing is not to her liking. (p. 159)

On her journey to find the blacksmith, Florens enters a community of Puritans. Her experience with them illustrates the role of religion in the production, circulation, and internalization of racist ideology. The Puritans persecute a young girl in their community named Daughter Jane whom they believe to be possessed by demons, and they shame Florens by making a spectacle of her black body. Associating her dark skin with the imagery they attach to Satan – a figure they call the Black Man – they look upon her as if she is another species altogether. Recalling their gaze, Florens feels her humanity slip away, and she understands her tenuous status. Her freedom and identity depend upon the symbolic protection – the letter from Rebekka – she carries:

> I walk alone except for the eyes that join me on my journey. Eyes that do not recognize me, eyes that examine me for a tail, an extra teat, a man's whip between my legs. . . . Inside I am shrinking. I climb the streambed under watching trees and know I am not the same. I am losing something with every step I take. I can feel the drain. Something precious is leaving me. I a thing apart. With the letter I belong and am lawful. Without it I am a weak calf abandon by the herd, a turtle without shell, a minion with no telltale signs but a darkness I am born with,

outside, yes, but inside as well and the inside dark is small, feathered and toothy. (p. 115)

In the process of writing her story, Florens believes that she is explaining herself to the blacksmith. But she is also writing herself into being and asserting her autonomous identity as an enslaved black woman. Writing in a space that she has been forbidden to enter, she discovers that her story exceeds the confines of the man-made room. She recalls a conversation with the blacksmith that transpired before Jacob's death when the blacksmith questions received distinctions between slave and free: "You say you see slaves freer than free men. One is a lion in the skin of an ass. The other is an ass in the skin of a lion. That it is the withering inside that enslaves and opens the door for what is wild" (p. 160). But Florens disagrees, challenging the hierarchy that would lead him to believe that as a free man, he can impose categories and definitions upon her, an enslaved woman. Florens believes that it is the "withering," the soul crushing that one human being inflicts upon another, that threatens her freedom and her humanity. She asserts that her "withering" began when the Puritans examined her body. The "wildness" that led her to attack the blacksmith when he throws her out of his house was her attempt to reassert her humanity. He may be the lion "who thinks his mane is all," but as she has learned from Daughter Jane, she can be the "shelion who does not" (p. 160).

Florens fears that if the blacksmith cannot read her words, they will have no meaning, becoming little more than a random assortment of shapes. But she then realizes that her words belong to the natural world, and they connect her to a universe larger than the categories to which humans assign each other. As she puts it:

Perhaps these words need the air that is out in the world. Need to fly up then fall, fall like ash over acres of primrose and mallow. Over a turquoise lake, beyond the eternal hemlocks, through clouds cut by rainbow and flavor the soil of the earth. . . .

See? You are correct. A minha mae too. I am become wilderness but I am also Florens. In full. Unforgiven. Unforgiving. No ruth, my love. None. Hear me? Slave. Free. I last. (p. 161)

Through the words she has written, she has come to embody the contradictions of her existence. She can affirm her own definitions of the categories to which she has been assigned; from her perspective, she can occupy positions that would seem to exclude one another. Moreover, she affirms that she can be both wilderness and civilized, both free and enslaved.

The final section of the novel reads like a love letter from a minha mae to Florens. Told from her point of view, it recounts her justification for giving Florens away. The victim of sexual abuse at the hands of Senhor and Senhora D'Ortega and rape by the enslaved black men who were ordered to "break we in" (p. 163), a minha mae knows that she must find a way out for her daughter. As soon as she sees Florens's breasts begin to bud and recognizes her taste for pretty things – her "vice for shoes" (p. 162) – a minha mae realizes that for her there will be "no protection." As she knows: "To be female in this place is to be an open wound that cannot heal. Even if scars form, the festering is ever below" (p. 163).

Florens may never be able to forgive her mother for this apparent act of abandonment, but a minha mae had endured the atrocities of enslavement in West Africa, the perils of the middle passage, and the auction block in Barbados. In terms that remind us of *Beloved*, she remembers those who died at sea, and she recalls yearning for death herself. She knows what it means to have her body inspected as if she were an animal, and she can identify the moment when she lost her name, her country and her family and became merely "negrita:" "Language, dress, gods, dance, habits, decoration, song – all of it cooked together in the color of my skin" (p. 165). Moreover, she has failed to find solace in religion. The Reverend Father agrees to teach the slaves to read, and he tries to console her with promises of salvation in the afterlife, but he cannot keep her safe from the D'Ortegas.

When a minha mae reads Jacob's contempt for the D'Ortegas and their possessions on his face, she understands that he will be her daughter's best hope of freedom. She recognizes that she must seize this opportunity to save her daughter, even if means that she will never see her again. As she reflects: "I saw the tall man see you as a human child, not pieces of eight" (p. 166). Given the limited consolation religion provides her, she does not try to convince herself that the escape that Jacob represents is a miracle sent by God. For her, it is a small mercy one human extends to another, and for her, that is enough.

Notes

1 For a thorough discussion of *The Big Box, The Book of Mean People,* and the *Who's Got Game?* Series, see Chia-yen Ku, "Not Safe for the Nursery? – Toni Morrison's Storybooks for Children," *EurAmerica* 36.4 (December 2006): 613–649.

2 Chia-yen Ku provides a brief survey of these reviews in "Not Safe for the Nursery," p. 616. See also her interview with Rob Cappriccioso, "Toni Morrison's Challenge," July 25, 2003, http://sparkaction.org/node/487, April 17, 2012.

3 Toni Morrison and Slade Morrison, *The Big Box* (New York: Hyperion, 1999), p. 6. Subsequent references are to this edition.

4 Toni Morrison and Slade Morrison, *The Book of Mean People* (New York: Hyperion, 2002).

5 Toni Morrison and Slade Morrison, *Who's Got Game? The Ant or the Grasshopper?* (New York: Scribner, 2003a), p. 13. Subsequent references are to this edition.

6 http://mythfolklore.net/aesopica/oxford/70.htm, October 23, 2011.

7 Toni Morrison and Slade Morrison, *Who's Got Game? The Lion or the Mouse?* (New York: Scribner, 2003b), p. 4. Subsequent references are to this edition.

8 http://mythfolklore.net/aesopica/perry/176.htm, October 23, 2011.

9 Toni Morrison and Slade Morrison, *Who's Got Game? Poppy or the Snake?* (New York: Scribner, 2003c), p. 2. Subsequent references are to this edition.

10 Toni Morrison, *Remember: The Journey to School Integration* (Boston: Houghton Mifflin, 2004), p. iii.

11 It becomes clear later in the book that several of these images are cropped from the same photograph. For example, the black and the white girl in profile are sitting across from each other in an integrated classroom. The white woman in profile is a teacher reading aloud to an integrated group of students of which the young white boy looking into the camera is one.

12 "Foreword" to *Love* by Toni Morrison (New York: Vintage, 2005), p. x. Subsequent references are to this edition.

13 Jean Wyatt, "*Love's* Time and the Reader: Ethical Effects of Nachtraglichkeit in Toni Morrison's *Love.*" *Narrative* 16.2 (May 2008): 193–221.

14 Idagay is a language the girls developed, similar to Pig Latin, in which the speaker moves the initial consonant or consonant blend to the end of a word and follows it with the letters "idagay." Thus, when Christine tells Heed: "Ou-yidagay a ave-slidagay," she is saying: "You a slave!" (p. 188).

15   For example, after her one extramarital affair, she believes she is pregnant when she is, in fact, menopausal.

16   *A minha mae* is the Portuguese phrase meaning "my mother" that Florens uses to refer to her mother.

17   "Toni Morrison Discusses *A Mercy*" with Lynn Neary. National Public Radio Book Tour. October 27, 2008. http://www.npr.org/templates/story/story.php?storyId=95961382

18   I have in mind moments such as Jacob Vaark's journey to Jublio, Senhor D'Ortega's plantation, Rebekka Vaark's arrival in America, and Florens's and Lina's arrival at the Vaark farm, to mention but a few examples.

19   "Toni Morrison Discusses *A Mercy.*"

Epilogue: *Home*

Home (2012), Morrison's 10th novel, reprises several of the techniques and themes we find in her earlier work. The story unfolds from multiple narrative perspectives, and Frank Money, one of the two central characters, occasionally speaks directly to, and corrects, the authorial presence. The writing is elegant, spare, poetic, and yet colloquial. Moreover, the novel reflects upon the power of memory and forgetting; the impact of social and political change on families and on individual lives; the vulnerability of children, especially young black girls in an environment dominated by racism, misogyny, and economic inequality; the mixed promise of migration. Like all of Morrison's novels, *Home* is concerned with reclaiming and retelling a period from the American past from the perspective of those who have largely been written out of that history. Furthermore, as the title suggests, the novel provides a meditation on the idea of home.[1]

As we have seen, throughout Morrison's fiction, houses and homes frequently function as metaphors for the dilemmas her characters face. To mention only a few, recall the repurposed storefront where the outcast Breedloves live; l'Arbe de la Croix, the grand, gaudy, grim and ill-constructed home that shelters the Streets, the Childs, and their secrets; 124, haunted by the ghost of Sethe's slain daughter; the great house that metaphorically kills Jacob Vaark. As Hilton Als observes in his now classic *New Yorker* essay, "Ghosts in the House," "Love and

Toni Morrison: Writing the Moral Imagination, First Edition. Valerie Smith.
© 2012 Valerie Smith. Published 2014 by John Wiley & Sons, Ltd.

disaster and all the other forms of human incident accumulate in Morrison's fictional houses."[2]

Home invites readers to think not so much about the significance of literal houses, but rather, about the broader meaning of home. More specifically, it asks us to think about the meaning of home during the 1950s, a decade for which many late twentieth- and twenty-first century Americans have become nostalgic. Contemporary US culture often associates the 1950s with an idealized vision of postwar prosperity and intact nuclear families and evinces a fascination with the fashion, architecture, and design of the period. Indeed, despite its association with the waning days of Jim Crow segregation, African Americans will also often romanticize this period as a time when black communities were more unified both socially and politically, and when people watched out for each other's children. Within the context of the failure of public education in this country and the broken promise of the 1954 Brown vs. Board of Education of Topeka decision, some will even yearn for a return to the pre-Brown era as a time when primary and secondary schools were safer, and public education was more effective. *Home* suggests that these idealized images of the 1950s depend upon a willed act of forgetting the complexities and contradictions of the period. In this novel, Morrison revisits that era in order to reflect on the complicated ways disenfranchised African Americans might have experienced it. By examining the idea of home from a variety of perspectives, she casts the '50s as a time when the notion of home was under assault.

Set in the immediate aftermath of the Korean War, *Home* focuses on the relationship between a brother and sister, Frank and Ycidra (or Cee) Money, separated when Frank joined the Army and went off to fight in Korea. After Frank (reminiscent of Shadrack from *Sula*) returns from the war plagued by hallucinations and other manifestations of what would now be called posttraumatic stress syndrome, he intends to remain in Seattle. But he undertakes his cross-country journey when he receives a letter summoning him back to his hometown, Lotus, Georgia, to rescue Cee: "Come fast. She be dead if you tarry."[3]

Despite the sacrifices he has made for his country, Frank is treated as worthless once he returns to the United States and begins to travel from Seattle to Lotus. Not only is he the victim of or witness to racial violence, harassment, and exclusion whether in the North or in the South, but his status as a veteran is of no consequence. Even Reverend

Jessie Maynard, the African American minister who offers him food, clothing, and money in Portland to help him on his way, treats him with contempt, seeing him as a sexual threat to his daughters rather than a man deserving of respect. As the narrator observes, "The Reverend was devoted to the needy, apparently, but only if they were properly clothed and not a young, hale, and very tall veteran" (p. 22). Afraid of being arrested for vagrancy if he is found standing or walking outside with no apparent purpose, forbidden entry to public restrooms, waiting rooms, and hotels, he is unwelcome in the country he risked his life to defend.[4] The country to which he returned is not his home.

The Korean War looms large in this book and constitutes an apt metaphor for the act of forgetting. Often called the Forgotten War because it was so poorly understood in its own time, it has been overshadowed in American cultural memory by the grand campaigns and legendary heroism of World War II and the dramatic divisions spawned by the Vietnam War. Frank is tormented by his memories of his friends' violent deaths and the murders he committed during the war; the narrative is haunted by flashbacks of scenes he desperately tries to forget. Moreover, the way in which Frank's service is so easily forgotten or dismissed points to the difficulty military veterans face when they return to the United States so deeply transformed by their experiences that they can no longer find a place where they belong.

The novel opens with Frank's memory of a time in his childhood when he and Cee wandered a few miles from home to watch the horses at a stud farm. On their way home, they are forced to hide when they see a group of men empty a black man's body into a hole in the ground and then bury it. Although they arrive home later than expected, the adults do not even notice them, because they are deep in discussion about "some disturbance" (p. 5).

Morrison does not explicitly identify the men as white and the scene that Frank and Cee witness as the aftermath of a lynching, but it is clear that that is what it is. The bucolic scene of childhood fascination turned suddenly dangerous, the black body disappeared on a country road, the adults back home so deeply lost in conversation that they do not even notice the children, all remind us of literary and oral narrative accounts of lynchings. As a pivotal, defining childhood memory, it speaks volumes about the sense of danger and instability that is wrapped up in Frank's ideas of nature and of home.

When he was 4, Frank, the rest of the Money family, and the 14 other black families in his community were forced to leave their homes in Bandera County, Texas under threat of death, driven out by a band of whites who want their land. The one elderly man who refuses to leave is beaten to death "just after dawn at the twenty-fourth hour." The "fleeing neighbors" who sneak back to bury him report that his eyes have been cut out (p. 10).

Frank, Cee, and their family are forced to move in with their grandfather and Lenore, their step-grandmother, in Lotus until they can save enough money to rent a place of their own. Here the children do not encounter loving, caring grandparents. Lenore condescends to her neighbors and family because of the money she inherited from her late husband. She especially despises Cee, the child born on the road from Texas to Lotus, because of her lowly origins, referring to her as "gutter child" (p. 45). Out of their abandonment and pain, Frank and Cee grow to depend on each other and forge a mutually sustaining relationship.

In search of a world larger than the stifling environment of Lotus – a world with *"no future, just long stretches of killing time"* (p. 83) – Frank enlists in the army to fight in Korea. With her brother gone, Cee is at a loss; to escape Lotus, she runs away to Atlanta with a man named Prince (short for Principal), who wants her only because she has a car. After he abandons her in Atlanta, Cee finds work with a physician, Dr. Beauregard Scott. At first, she is mightily impressed by his beautiful home and the office in which he works, the abundance of food, and the comfortable bed to sleep in. But this home, too, turns poisonous. She quickly goes from being Scott's assistant to being the victim of this eugenicist who experiments on the reproductive organs of poor black women. By the time Frank rescues her and takes her back to Lotus, Dr. Scott has rendered her infertile and has almost taken her life.

When they were children, Frank could calm Cee's fears simply by placing one hand on her head and the other at the nape of her neck. By the end of the novel, both realize that their respective traumas will be healed not by obliterating the pain of the past, but by facing their fears together. In the end, both Frank and Cee find healing and find home. Cee's body is healed by the ministrations of the community of women in Lotus, and her soul begins to recover when she faces how deeply she feels her inability to bear children. She also begins to quilt, an expression of her creativity that enables her to transform scraps into a product that is both beautiful and functional. Frank's spirit begins to heal when he acknowledges that he who loves his own little sister so deeply, had killed a young Korean girl in order to destroy the part of him that was tempted to respond to her sexually. For both together, it means retrieving the bones of the victim of the lynch mob, wrapping them in Cee's quilt, and giving them a proper and respectful burial. By reclaiming their personal secrets, they are able to reclaim Lotus as their literal, physical home. Through their willingness to confront their past, they find their true home within them in the memories they share.

In her 1997 essay entitled "Home," Morrison observes that since she had to live in a "racial house," a world already constructed out of racialized power relations and discursive practices, as a writer she was free to "redecorate, redesign, even reconceive the racial house" into a "home of her own."[5] She remarks that all of her work has been troubled by this question: "How to be free and situated; how to convert a racist house into a race-specific, yet nonracist home" (p. 5). This domesticating project runs throughout her oeuvre, enabling her to reanimate and reframe the past through the stories of the losses and aspirations, despair, and desires of those who have been written out of history. This question lies at the heart of *Home* as well. Frank and Cee move from one house to another, encountering the codes and exclusions of the landscape of 1950s America in the search for a home. The bonds of shared memories and experience reverse their migrations and equip them with the love, courage, and creativity they require to make a home for themselves and for each other within their father's (and mother's) house.

Notes

1 See, for example, Tayari Jones, "*Home*, by Toni Morrison: Review," *SFGate*.com, May 6, 2012, http://www.sfgate.com/cgibin/article.cgi? f=/c/a/2012/05/04/RVMH1O4I6A.DT (accessed May 13, 2012); Michiko Kakutani, "Soldier Is Defeated by War Abroad, Then Welcomed Back by Racism," *New York Times*, May 7, 2012, http://www.nytimes.com/2012/05/08/books/home-a-novel-by-toni-morrison.html?_r=1&ref=michikokakutani (accessed May 13, 2012); Nisha Lilia Diu, "*Home* by Toni

Morrison: Review," *The Telegraph,* May 10, 2012, http://www.telegraph. co.uk/culture/books/fictionreviews/9246047/Home-by-Toni-Morrison-review.html (accessed May 13, 2012); Leah Hager Cohen, "Point of Return," *The New York Times Book Review,* May 17, 2012, http://www.nytimes. com/2012/05/20/books/review/home-a-novel-by-toni-morrison.html (accessed May 18, 2012).

2   Hilton Als, "Ghosts in the House: How Toni Morrison Fostered a Generation of Black Writers." *The New Yorker* 79.32 (October 27, 2003): 64.

3   Toni Morrison, *Home* (New York: Knopf, 2012), p. 8. Subsequent references will be to this edition.

4   To mention but a few examples: Mrs. Locke gives Frank a bag of food when he leaves her house in Seattle because she knows he will not be able to eat at a bus stop counter. Reverend Maynard copies the names and addresses of rooming houses and hotels where he can stay from Green's guide for black travelers. And on the train between Portland and Chicago, he rides with a man who is beaten by a crowd of whites for trying to enter a station waiting room, and his wife who is beaten for trying to help him.

5   Toni Morrison, "Home," p. 4.

Further Reading

Abel, Elizabeth. "Black Writing, White Reading: Race and the Politics of Feminist Interpretation." *Critical Inquiry* 19:3 (Spring 1993), 470–498.

Aguiar, Sarah Appleton. "Passing on Death: Stealing Life in Toni Morrison's *Paradise.*" *African American Review* 38 (Fall 2004), 513–519.

Andrews, William L. and Nellie Y. McKay, eds. *Beloved: A Casebook.* New York: Oxford University Press, 1999.

Ashe, Bertram D. "'Why Don't He Like My Hair?': Constructing African-American Standards of Beauty in Toni Morrison's *Song of Solomon.*" *African American Review* 29:4 (Winter 1995), 579–593.

Bouson, J. Brooks. *Quiet as It's Kept: Shame, Trauma, and Race in the Novels of Toni Morrison.* New York: State University of New York Press, 2000.

Dalsgard, Katrine. "'The One All-Black Town Worth the Pain': American Exceptionalism, Historical Narration, and the Critique of Nationhood in Toni Morrison's *Paradise.*" *African American Review* 35 (Summer 2001), 233–248.

Fallon, Robert. "Music and the Allegory of Memory in *Margaret Garner.*" *Modern Fiction Studies* 52:2 (Summer 2006), 524–541.

Feng, Pin-cha. "'We Was Girls Together': The Double Female Bildungsroman in Toni Morrison's *Love.*" *Feminist Studies in English Literature* 15.2 (Winter 2007), 37–63.

Ferguson, Rebecca. "History, Memory and Language in Toni Morrison's *Beloved.*" In *Feminist Criticism: Theory and Practice,* edited by Susan Sellers, 109–127. Toronto, Canada: University of Toronto Press, 1991.

Furman, Jan. *Toni Morrison's Fiction.* Columbia, SC: University of South Carolina Press, 1996.

Toni Morrison: Writing the Moral Imagination, First Edition. Valerie Smith.
© 2012 Valerie Smith. Published 2014 by John Wiley & Sons, Ltd.

Gascuena Gahete, Javier. "Narrative Delusion and Aesthetic Pleasure in Toni Morrison's *Love.*" In *Figures of Belatedness: Postmodernist Fiction in English*, edited by Javier Gascuena Gahete and Paula Martin Salvan, 259–273. Cordoba, Spain: Servicio de Publicaciones, Universidad de Cordoba, 2006.

Gates, Henry Louis Jr. and Kwame Anthony Appiah, eds. *Toni Morrison: Critical Perspectives Past and Present*. New York: Amistad, 1993.

Gauthier, Marni. "The Other Side of Paradise: Toni Morrison's (Un)Making of Mythic History." *African American Review* 39 (Fall 2005), 395–414.

Grandt, Jurgen E. "Kinds of Blue: Toni Morrison, Hans Janowitz and the Jazz Aesthetic." *African American Review* 38 (Summer 2004), 303–322.

Heinze, Denise. *The Dilemma of "Double-Consciousness:" Toni Morrison's Novels*. Athens, GA: The University of Georgia Press, 1995.

Henderson, Mae G. "Toni Morrison's *Beloved*: Re-Membering the Body as Historical Text." In *Comparative American Identities*, edited by Hortense Spillers, 62–86. New York: Routledge, 1991.

Hogue, W. Lawrence. "Postmodernism, Traditional Cultural Forms, and the African American Narrative: Major's *Reflex*, Morrison's *Jazz*, and Reed's *Mumbo Jumbo.*" *Novel: A Forum on Fiction* 35 2/3 (Spring–Summer 2002), 169–192.

Horvitz, Deborah. "Nameless Ghosts: Possession and Dispossession in *Beloved.*" *American Literature* 17 (1989), 157–167.

House, Elizabeth. "Toni Morrison's Ghost: The Beloved Who Is Not Beloved." *Studies in American Fiction* 18 (1990), 17–26.

Ikard, David. *Breaking the Silence: Toward a Black Male Feminist Criticism*. Baton Rouge, IL: Louisiana State University Press, 2007.

Jenkins, Candace M. "Pure Black: Class, Color, and Intraracial Politics in Toni Morrison's *Paradise.*" *Modern Fiction Studies* 52:2 (July 2006), 270–296.

Jennings, Lavinia Delois. "*A Mercy*: Toni Morrison Plots the Formation of Racial Slavery in Seventeenth-Century America." *Callaloo* 32:2 (Spring 2009), 645–649.

Khayati, Abdellatif. "Representation, race, and the 'Language' of the Ineffable in Toni Morrison's Narrative." *African American Review* 33:2 (Summer 1999), 313–324.

King, Lovalerie and Lynn Orilla Scott, eds. *James Baldwin and Toni Morrison: Comparative Critical and Theoretical Essays*. New York: Palgrave Macmillan, 2006.

Krumholz, Linda J. "Reading and Insight in Toni Morrison's *Paradise.*" *African American Review* 36 (Spring 2002), 395–408.

McKay, Nellie Y., ed. *Critical Essays on Toni Morrison*. Boston, MA: G. K. Hall, 1998.

Michael, Magali Comier. "Re-Imagining Agency: Toni Morrison's *Paradise.*" *African American Review* 36 (Winter 2002), 643–661.

Middleton, David. *Toni Morrison's Fiction: Contemporary Criticism*. New York: Garland Publishing, 2000.

Morrison, Toni. "City Limits, Village Values: Concepts of the Neighborhood in Black Fiction." In *Literature and the Urban Experience*, edited by Michael C. Jaye and Ann Chalmers Watts, 35–43. New Brunswick, NJ: Rutgers University Press, 1981.

Morrison, Toni. "Memory, Creation, and Writing." *Thought* 59:235 (December 1984), 385–390.

Morrison, Toni. "Black Matters." *Grand Street* 10:4 (1991), 205–225.

Morrison, Toni. "How Can Values Be Taught in the University?" *Michigan Quarterly Review* 40:2 (Spring 2001), 273–278.

Moses, Cat. "The Blues Aesthetic in Toni Morrison's *The Bluest Eye*." *African American Review* 33 (Winter 1999), 623–637.

Page, Philip. *Dangerous Freedom: Fusion and Fragmentation in Toni Morrison's Novels*. Jackson, MS: University Press of Mississippi, 1995.

Page, Philip. "Furrowing All the Brows: Interpretation and the Transcendent in Toni Morrison's *Paradise*." *African American Review* 35 (Winter 2001), 639–651.

Peterson, Nancy J., ed. *Toni Morrison: Critical and Theoretical Approaches*. Baltimore, MD: The Johns Hopkins University Press, 1997.

Peterson, Nancy J. "Introduction: On Incendiary Art, the Moral Imagination, and Toni Morrison." *Modern Fiction Studies* 52:2 (July 2006), 261–269.

Powers, Christopher. "The Third Eye: Love, Memory, and History in Toni Morrison's *Beloved, Jazz* and *Paradise*." In *Narrating the Past: (Re)Constructing Memory, (Re)Negotiating History*, edited by Nandita Batra and Vartan P. Messier, 31–37. Newcastle upon Tyne, England: Cambridge Scholars, 2007.

Robolin, Stephane. "Loose Memory in Toni Morrison's *Paradise* and Zoe Wicomb's *David's Story*." *Modern Fiction Studies* 52:2 (July 2006), 297–320.

Romero, Channette. "Creating the Beloved Community: Race and Nation in Toni Morrison's *Paradise*." *African American Review* 39:3 (Fall 2005), 415–430.

Stave, Shirley A., ed. *Toni Morrison and the Bible: Contested Intertextualities*. New York: Peter Lang Publishing, 2006.

Sweeney, Megan. "Racial House, Big House, Home: Contemporary Abolitionism in Toni Morrison's *Paradise*." *Meridians* 4:2 (2004), 40–67.

Sweeney, Megan. "'Something Rogue:' Commensurability, Commodification, Crime and Justice in Toni Morrison's Latest Fiction." *Modern Fiction Studies* 52:2 (July 2006), 440–469.

Tally, Justine. *Paradise Reconsidered: Toni Morrison's (Hi)stories and Truths*. Hamburg, Germany: Lit Verlag, 1999.

Waegner, Cathy Covell. "Ruthless Epic Footsteps: Shoes, Migrants, and the Settlement of the Americas in Toni Morrison's *A Mercy*." In *Post-National*

Enquiries: Essays on Ethnic and Racial Border Crossings, edited by Jopi Nyman, 91–112. Newcastle upon Tyne, England: Cambridge Scholars Publishing, 2009.

Wallace, Kathleen R. and Karla Armbruster. "The Novels of Toni Morrison: Wild Wilderness Where There was None." In *Beyond Nature Writing: Expanding the Boundaries of Ecocriticism,* edited by Kathleen R. Wallace and Karla Armbruster, 211–230. Charlottesville, VA: University Press of Virginia, 1997.

Wallace, Maurice. "Print, Prosthesis, Impersonation: Toni Morrison's *Jazz* and the Limits of American Literary History." *American Literary History* 20:4 (Winter 2008), 794–806.

Wilentz, Gay. "Civilizations Underneath: African Heritage as Cultural Discourse in Toni Morrison's *Song of Solomon.*" *African American Review* 26:1 (Spring 1992), 61–77.

Willis, Sharese Terrell. "Eruptions of Funk: Historicizing Toni Morrison." *Black American Literature Forum* 16:1 (Spring 1982), 34–42.

Wyatt, Jean. "Giving Body to the Word: The Maternal Symbolic in Toni Morrison's *Beloved.*" *Publications of the Modern Language Association* 108:3 (May 1993), 474–486.

Yoo, JaeEun. "The Site of Murder: Textual Space and Ghost Narrator in Toni Morrison's *Love.*" In *Space, Haunting, Discourse,* edited by Maria Holmgren Troy and Elisabeth Wenno, 153–167. Newcastle upon Tyne, England: Cambridge Scholars Press, 2008.

Works Cited

Als, Hilton. "Ghosts in the House: How Toni Morrison Fostered a Generation of Black Writers." *The New Yorker* 79.32 (October 27, 2003), 64–75.

Aubry, Timothy. "Beware the Furrow of the Middlebrow: Searching for *Paradise* on *The Oprah Winfrey Show*." In *The Oprah Affect: Critical Essays on Oprah's Book Club*, edited by Cecilia Konchar Farr and Jaime Harker, 163–188. Albany, NY: State University of New York Press, 2008.

Baker, Houston A. Jr. *Modernism and the Harlem Renaissance*. Chicago, IL: University of Chicago Press, 1989.

Bell, Bernard. *The Afro-American Novel and Its Tradition*. Amherst, MA: University of Massachusetts Press, 1987.

Berger, James. "Ghosts of Liberalism: Morrison's *Beloved* and the Moynihan Report." *Publications of the Modern Language Association* 111:3 (1996), 408–420.

Blake, Susan L. "Toni Morrison." In *Dictionary of Literary Biography, Vol. 33, Afro-American Fiction Writers after 1955*, edited by Thadious M. Davis and Trudier Harris, 187–199. Detroit, MI: Gale Research Co., 1984.

Brenkman, John. "Politics and Form in *Song of Solomon*." *Social Text* 39 (Summer 1994), 57–82.

Brown, Caroline. "Golden Gray and the Talking Book: Identity as a Site of Artful Construction in Toni Morrison's *Jazz*." *African American Review* 36:4 (Winter 2002), 629–642.

Christian, Barbara. " 'The Past Is Infinite': History and Myth in Toni Morrison's Trilogy." *Social Identities* 6:4 (2000), 411–423.

Conner, Marc C., ed. *The Aesthetics of Toni Morrison: Speaking the Unspeakable*. Jackson, MS: University Press of Mississippi, 2000.

Toni Morrison: Writing the Moral Imagination, First Edition. Valerie Smith.
© 2012 Valerie Smith. Published 2014 by John Wiley & Sons, Ltd.

Darling, Marsha. "'In the Realm of Responsibility:' A Conversation with Toni Morrison." In *Conversations with Toni Morrison*, edited by Danille Taylor-Guthrie, 246–254. Jackson, MS: University Press of Mississippi, 1994.

Davidson, Robert. "Racial Stock and 8-Rocks: Communal Historiography in Toni Morrison's *Paradise*." *Twentieth Century Literature* 47:3 (Fall 2001), 335–373.

Davis, Cynthia A. "Self, Society, and Myth in Toni Morrison's Fiction." *Contemporary Literature* 23:3 (Summer 1982), 323–342.

Denard, Carolyn, ed. *Toni Morrison: What Moves at the Margin, Selected Nonfiction*. Jackson, MS: University Press of Mississippi, 2008.

Douglas, Ann. *Terrible Honesty: Mongrel Manhattan in the 1920s*. New York: Farrar, Straus and Giroux, 1995.

Duvall, John N. *The Identifying Fictions of Toni Morrison*. New York: Palgrave, 2000.

Fullilove, Mindy. *Root Shock: How Tearing Up City Neighborhoods Hurts America and What We Can Do about It*. New York: Random House, 2004.

Fultz, Lucille P. *Toni Morrison: Playing with Difference*. Urbana, IL: University of Illinois Press, 2003.

Gillespie, Diane and Missy Dehn Kubitschek. "Who Cares? Women-Centered Psychology in *Sula*." In *Toni Morrison's Fiction: Contemporary Criticism*, edited by David Middleton, 61–91. New York: Garland Publishing, 2000.

Goldsby, Jacqueline. *A Spectacular Secret: Lynching in American Life and Literature*. Chicago, IL: University of Chicago Press, 2006.

Hirsch, Marianne. "'Knowing Their Names': Toni Morrison's *Song of Solomon*." In *New Essays on Song of Solomon*, edited by Valerie Smith, 69–92. New York: Cambridge University Press, 1995.

Holloway, Karla F. C. "*Beloved:* A Spiritual." In *Beloved: A Casebook*, edited by William L. Andrews and Nellie Y. McKay, 67–78. New York: Oxford University Press, 1999.

Johnson, Barbara. "'Aesthetic' and 'Rapport' in Toni Morrison's *Sula*." In *The Aesthetics of Toni Morrison: Speaking the Unspeakable*, edited by Marc C. Conner, 3–11. Jackson, MS: University Press of Mississippi, 2000.

Jones, Jessie W. and Audrey Vinson. "An Interview with Toni Morrison." In *Conversations with Toni Morrison*, edited by Danille Taylor Guthrie, 171–187. Jackson, MS: University Press of Mississippi, 1994.

Keizer, Arlene R. *Black Subjects: Identity Formation in the Contemporary Narrative of Slavery*. New York: Cornell University Press, 2004.

Khaleghi, Mahboobeh. "Narration and Intertextuality in Toni Morrison's *Jazz*." *The Criterion: An International Journal in English* 2:1 (April 2011), 1–10.

Krumholz, Linda. "The Ghosts of Slavery: Historical Recovery in Toni Morrison's *Beloved*." *African American Review* 26 (Autumn 1992), 395–408.

Ku, Chia-yen. "Not Safe for the Nursery? – Toni Morrison's Storybooks for Children." *EurAmerica* 36:4 (December 2006), 613–649.

LaCapra, Dominick. *Writing History, Writing Trauma*. Baltimore, MD: Johns Hopkins University Press, 2001.

LeClair, Thomas. "The Language Must Not Sweat: A Conversation with Toni Morrison." In *Conversations with Toni Morrison*, edited by Danille Taylor-Guthrie, 119–128. Jackson, MS: University Press of Mississippi, 1994.

Lee, Catherine Carr. "The South in Toni Morrison's *Song of Solomon:* Initiation, Healing and Home." *Studies in the Literary Imagination* 3:2 (Fall 1998), 109–124.

Lee, Dorothy H. "*Song of Solomon:* To Ride the Air." *Black American Literature Forum* 16:2 (Summer 1982), 64–70.

Lesoinne, Veronique. "Answer Jazz's Call: Experiencing Toni Morrison's *Jazz*." *Multi-Ethnic Literature of the U.S.* 22:3 (Autumn 1997), 157–166.

Lubiano, Wahneema H. "The Postmodernist Rag: Political Identity and the Vernacular in *Song of Solomon*." In *New Essays on Song of Solomon*, edited by Valerie Smith, 93–116. New York: Cambridge University Press, 1995.

Lubiano, Wahneema H., ed. *The House That Race Built: Black Americans, U. S. Terrain*. New York: Pantheon, 1997.

Ludwig, Sami. "Toni Morrison's Social Criticism." In *The Cambridge Companion to Toni Morrison*, edited by Justine Tally, 125–138. Cambridge, UK: Cambridge University Press, 2008.

Mandel, Naomi. " 'I Made the Ink:' Identity, Complicity, 60 Million, and More." *Modern Fiction Studies* 48:3 (Fall 2002), 581–613.

Menand, Louis. "The War between Men and Women." Review of *Paradise*, by Toni Morrison. *The New Yorker*, January 12, 1998, 78–82.

McBride, Dwight. "Toni Morrison, Intellectual." In *The Cambridge Companion to Toni Morrison*, edited by Justine Tally, 162–174. Cambridge, UK: Cambridge University Press, 2008.

McDowell, Deborah E. " 'The Self and the Other': Reading Toni Morrison's *Sula* and the Black Female Text." In *Critical Essays on Toni Morrison*, edited by Nellie Y. McKay, 77–89. Boston, MA: G. K. Hall, 1988.

Medoro, Dana. "Justice and Citizenship in Toni Morrison's *Song of Solomon*." *Canadian Review of American Studies* 32:1 (2002), 1–16.

Mitchell, Angelyn. " 'Sth, I Know that Woman': History, Gender, and the South in Toni Morrison's *Jazz*." *Studies in the Literary Imagination* 31:2 (Fall 1998), 49–60.

Morrison, Toni. *The Bluest Eye*. New York: Holt, Rinehart and Winston, 1970; rpt. New York: Plume, 1973.

Morrison, Toni. *Sula*. New York: Knopf, 1973; rpt. New York: Vintage, 2004.

Morrison, Toni. *Song of Solomon*. New York: Vintage, 1977.

Morrison, Toni. *Tar Baby*. New York: Plume, 1982; rpt. New York: Vintage 2004.

Morrison, Toni. "Recitatif." In *Confirmation: An Anthology of African American Women*, edited by Imamu Amiri Baraka and Amina Baraka, New York: William Morrow, 1983.

Morrison, Toni. "Rootedness: The Ancestor as Foundation." In *Black Women Writers (1950–1980): A Critical Evaluation*, edited by Mari Evans, 339–345. New York: Doubleday, Anchor Books, 1984a.

Morrison, Toni. "Memory, Creation, and Writing." *Thought: A Review of Culture and Ideas* 59 (December 1984b), 385–390.

Morrison, Toni. "The Site of Memory." In *Inventing the Truth: The Art and Craft of Memoir*, edited by William Zinsser, 183–200. Boston, MA: Houghton Mifflin, 1987a.

Morrison, Toni. *Beloved*. New York: Knopf, 1987b.

Morrison, Toni. "Unspeakable Things Unspoken: The Afro-American Presence in American Literature." *Michigan Quarterly Review* 28:1 (1989), 1–34.

Morrison, Toni. *Jazz*. New York: Knopf, 1992.

Morrison, Toni. *Playing in the Dark: Whiteness and the Literary Imagination*. Cambridge, MA: Harvard University Press, 1992a.

Morrison, Toni, ed. *Race-ing Justice, En-gendering Power: Essays on Anita Hill, Clarence Thomas, and the Construction of Reality*. New York: Pantheon Books, 1992b.

Morrison, Toni. *The Nobel Lecture in Literature, 1993*. New York: Alfred A. Knopf, 1993.

Morrison, Toni. *Home*. New York: Knopf, 2012.

Morrison, Toni. "Home." In *House That Race Built: Black Americans, U. S. Terrain*, edited by Wahneema H. Lubiano, 3–12. New York: Pantheon, 1997.

Morrison, Toni. *Paradise*. New York: Knopf, 1998.

Morrison, Toni. *Remember: The Journey to School Integration*. Boston, MA: Houghton Mifflin, 2004.

Morrison, Toni. *Love*. New York: Vintage, 2005.

Morrison, Toni. *A Mercy*. New York: Vintage, 2008.

Morrison, Toni. "Rediscovering Black History." In *What Moves at the Margin: Selected Nonfiction*, edited by Carolyn C. Denard, 39–55. Jackson, MS: University Press of Mississippi, 2008a.

Morrison, Toni. "The Dancing Mind." In *Toni Morrison: What Moves at the Margin: Selected Nonfiction*, edited by Carolyn C. Denard, 187–190. Jackson, MS: University Press of Mississippi, 2008b.

Morrison, Toni and Claudia Brodsky Lacour, eds. *Birth of a Nation'hood: Gaze, Script and Spectacle in the O. J. Simpson Trial*. New York: Pantheon Books, 1997.

Morrison, Toni and Slade Morrison. *The Big Box*. New York: Hyperion, 1999.

Morrison, Toni and Slade Morrison. *The Book of Mean People*. New York: Hyperion, 2002.

Morrison, Toni and Slade Morrison. *Who's Got Game? The Ant or the Grasshopper?* New York: Scribner, 2003a.

Morrison, Toni and Slade Morrison. *Who's Got Game? The Lion or the Mouse?* New York: Scribner, 2003b.

Morrison, Toni and Slade Morrison. *Who's Got Game? Poppy or the Snake?* New York: Scribner, 2003c.

Morrison, Toni, Gayatri Spivak, and Ngahuia Te Awekotuku. "Guest Column: Roundtable on the Future of the Humanities in a Fragmented World." *Publications of the Modern Language Association* 120 (2005), 715–723.

Naylor, Gloria and Toni Morrison. "A Conversation." *Southern Review* 21 (July 1985), 567–593.

North, Michael. *The Dialect of Modernism: Race, Language, and Twentieth-Century Literature*. New York: Oxford University Press, 1998.

Page, Philip. "Traces of Derrida in Toni Morison's *Jazz*." *African American Review* 29:1 (Spring 1995), 55–66.

Perry, Michael. "Resisting *Paradise*: Toni Morrison, Oprah Winfrey, and the Middlebrow Audience." In *The Oprah Affect: Critical Essays on Oprah's Book Club*, edited by Cecilia Konchar Farr and Jaime Harker, 119–140. Albany, NY: State University of New York Press, 2008.

Riding, Alan. "Rap and Film at the Louvre? What's Up with That?" *The New York Times*, November 21, 2006. Web May 2, 2010.

Rody, Caroline. "Toni Morrison's *Beloved*: History, 'Rememory,' and a 'Clamor for a Kiss.'" *American Literary History* 7 (Spring 1995), 92–119.

Rody, Caroline. "Impossible Voices: Ethnic Postmodern Narration in Toni Morrison's *Jazz* and Karen Tei Yamashita's *Through the Arc of the Rain Forest*." *Contemporary Literature* 41:4 (2000), 618–641.

Rody, Caroline. *The Daughter's Return: African American and Caribbean Women's Fictions of History*. New York: Oxford University Press, 2001.

Rudwick, Eliott. *Race Riot at East St. Louis: July 2, 1917*. Urbana, IL: University of Illinois Press, 1982.

Rushdy, Ashraf H. A. *The Neo-Slave Narrative: Studies in the Social Logic of a Literary Form*. New York: Oxford University Press, 1999.

Rushdy, Ashraf H. A. *Remembering Generations: Race and Family in Contemporary African American Fiction*. Chapel Hill, NC: University of North Carolina Press, 2001.

Scarry, Elaine. *The Body in Pain: The Making and Unmaking of the World*. New York: Oxford University Press, 1985.

Schappell, Elissa and Claudia Brodsky Lacour. "The Art of Fiction CXXXIV: Toni Morrison." *Paris Review* 35 (Fall 1993), 82–125.

Schreiber, Evelyn Jaffe. *Race, Trauma, and Home in the Novels of Toni Morrison.* Baton Rouge, LA: Louisiana State University Press, 2010.

Skerrett, Joseph T. Jr. "Recitation to the Griot: Storytelling and Listening in Toni Morrison's *Song of Solomon.*" In *Conjuring: Black Women, Fiction, and Literary Tradition*, edited by Marjorie Pryse and Hortense J. Spillers, 192–202. Bloomington, IN: Indiana University Press, 1985.

Smith, Valerie. "The Quest For and Discovery of Identity in Toni Morrison's *Song of Solomon.*" *Southern Review* 21:3 (Summer 1985), 721–732.

Stephens, Michelle. "The Harlem Renaissance: The New Negro at Home and Abroad." In *A Companion to African American Literature*, edited by Gene Andrew Jarrett, 212–226. Oxford: Wiley-Blackwell, 2010.

Stern, Katherine. "Toni Morrison's Beauty Formula." In *The Aesthetics of Toni Morrison: Speaking the Unspeakable*, edited by Marc C. Conner, 77–91. Jackson, MI: University Press of Mississippi, 2000.

Tally, Justine. "The Morrison Trilogy." In *The Cambridge Companion to Toni Morrison*, edited by Justine Tally, 75–91. New York: Cambridge University Press, 2007.

Thompson, Lisa. *Beyond the Black Lady: Sexuality and the New African American Middle Class.* Urbana and Chicago, IL: University of Illinois Press, 2009.

Treherne, Matthew. "Figuring In, Figuring Out: Narration and Negotiation in Toni Morrison's *Jazz.*" *Narrative* 11:2 (May 2003), 199–212.

Van Der Zee, James, Owen Dodson, and Camille Billops. *The Harlem Book of the Dead.* Dobbs Ferry, NY: Morgan and Morgan, 1978.

Walker, Melissa. *Down from the Mountaintop: Black Women's Novels in the Wake of the Civil Rights Movement, 1966–1989.* New Haven, CT: Yale University Press, 1991.

Wall, Cheryl A. "Toni Morrison, Editor and Teacher." In *The Cambridge Companion to Toni Morrison*, edited by Justine Tally, 139–150. Cambridge, UK: Cambridge University Press, 2008.

Weisenburger, Steven. *Modern Medea: A Family Story of Slavery and Child-Murder from the Old South.* New York: Hill and Wang, 1998.

Werner, Craig H. "The Briar Patch of Modernist Myth: Morrison, Barthes and *Tar Baby* As-Is." In *Critical Essays on Toni Morrison*, edited by Nellie Y. McKay, 150–167. Boston, MA: G. K. Hall, 1988.

Wyatt, Jean. "*Love's* Time and the Reader: Ethical Effects of Nachtraglichkeit in Toni Morrison's *Love.*" *Narrative* 16:2 (May 2008), 193–221.

Index

Note: page numbers in **bold** indicate major discussions of works.

Toni Morrison: Writing the Moral Imagination, First Edition. Valerie Smith.
© 2012 Valerie Smith. Published 2014 by John Wiley & Sons, Ltd.